Children Learn What They Live

Parenting to Inspire Values

by Dorothy Law Nolte
author of the classic poem
"Children Learn What They Live"
and Rachel Harris

Illustrations by Annette Cable

....

WORKMAN PUBLISHING • NEW YORK

Library of Congress Cataloging-in-Publication Data
Nolte, Dorothy
    Children learn what they live : parenting to inspire values /
by Dorothy Law Nolte and Rachel Harris.
    p. cm.
    ISBN-13: 978-0-7611-0919-8
    1. Parenting. 2. Parent and child. 3. Child rearing 4. Example.
I. Harris, Rachel. II. Title.
HQ755.8.N62   1998
649'.1—dc21   97-49243
                CIP

Workman books are available at special discounts when purchased in
bulk for premiums and sales promotions as well as for fund-raising or
educational use. Special editions or book excerpts can also be created
to specification. For details, contact the Special Sales Director at the
address below.

Workman Publishing Company, Inc.
225 Varick Street
New York, NY 10014-4381

Manufactured in the United States of America

First Printing May 1998
29 28 27

DEDICATION

*I dedicate this book in love and light
to all the children of life.*

—DOROTHY LAW NOLTE

*To my daughter, Ashley, who has taught
me about love and parenting.*

—RACHEL HARRIS

ACKNOWLEDGMENTS

Our heartfelt appreciation goes to our editor,
Margot Herrera, for her many contributions
and insights in the writing of this book.
We are also grateful to Janet Hulstrand
for her close attention and perceptive
additions to the manuscript. Warm thanks
to designer Nancy Gonzalez, as well as
to Bob Silverstein, our agent.

CONTENTS

Children Learn What They Live

If children live with criticism, they learn to condemn.

If children live with hostility, they learn to fight.

If children live with fear, they learn to be apprehensive.

If children live with pity, they learn to feel sorry for themselves.

If children live with ridicule, they learn to feel shy.

If children live with jealousy, they learn to feel envy.

If children live with shame, they learn to feel guilty.

If children live with encouragement, they learn confidence.

If children live with tolerance, they learn patience.

If children live with praise, they learn appreciation.

If children live with acceptance, they learn to love.

If children live with approval, they learn to like themselves.

If children live with recognition, they learn it is good to have a goal.

If children live with sharing, they learn generosity.

If children live with honesty, they learn truthfulness.

If children live with fairness, they learn justice.

If children live with kindness and consideration, they learn respect.

If children live with security, they learn to have faith in themselves and in those about them.

If children live with friendliness, they learn the world is a nice place in which to live.

—Dorothy Law Nolte

FOREWORD

by Jack Canfield,
Co-author, *Chicken Soup for the Soul*
and *Chicken Soup for the Mother's Soul*

Ifirst discovered "Children Learn What They Live" in the early seventies when I was writing a book on how to build children's self-esteem in the classroom. I instantly fell in love with the poem and reproduced it for all the teachers in the school where I taught. Every line seemed to contain a statement that I intuitively knew to be the truth. I was astounded that so much wisdom could be encapsulated in so few words.

It never occurred to me that I would ever meet the author of the poem, but several years later I did meet Dorothy, and her husband Claude, at a psychology conference. They graciously invited me to their room and treated me with all the acceptance, kindness, encouragement, and friendliness that Dorothy had written about in the poem. It was an evening I will never forget. I doubt they ever guessed how much influence their love and caring had had on a young educator who was struggling to learn to love himself and to teach his students to love and accept themselves, as well.

"Children Learn What They Live" served as a set of guiding principles for my interactions with my students and, later, my interactions with my three sons. As with all principles for living and parenting, they are easier to talk and write about than to put into daily practice.

In my thirty years as an educator and leader of parenting workshops, I have come to believe that most parents truly want to be loving, kind, compassionate, accepting, honest, and fair with their children. The problem is that most parents have never had a course in the specific methods and techniques of interaction, communication, and discipline that produce compassionate, caring, honest, and fair parenting.

No parent I have ever known wakes up in the morning, turns to his or her spouse and says, "I've just thought of four really great ways to destroy little Billy's self-esteem. We can judge him, ridicule him, shame him, and lie to him." Nobody ever sets out to purposely hurt their children, and yet parents often do just that. It's not intentional. It is usually out of unawareness and fear that parents pass on their own limited beliefs and emotional hang-ups to their children.

It takes an act of courage and consciousness to break the negative and destructive patterns that may unconsciously control our interactions with our children and to choose to live consciously and intentionally with the purpose of raising healthy, happy, and well-adjusted children.

In *Children Learn What They Live* Dorothy Law Nolte has taken each line of her classic poem and taught us all— through anecdotes and specific examples—how to put into daily action the valuable precepts it contains. She masterfully conveys, in simple and easy-to-understand language, how to be less critical and more tolerant, less judgmental and more accepting, less shaming and more encouraging, less hostile and more child-friendly.

You also get an extra bonus when you read this book: in addition to learning how to be a more effective parent, you will also learn how to be a better spouse, teacher, and manager. The principles and methods presented here are universal principles for bringing about loving, respectful, affirming, and empowering relationships with anyone. I firmly believe that if everyone practiced these principles in all of their relationships, there would be less violence and fewer wars, fewer strikes and more productivity in the workplace, less acting out and more time spent learning in the classroom. We'd have fewer people in prisons, on welfare, and in drug rehab centers. I encourage you to consider that most of the world's problems begin in the home, and by becoming a better parent, you are making the most solid contribution you can to solving the huge, seemingly intractable problems we face in the world today.

No matter how good a parent you currently are, you are about to embark on an adventure that will take you to the next level of magic. What could be more rewarding than knowing that you are becoming better able to raise children that are confident, assertive, patient, appreciative, loving, goal-oriented, generous, truthful, fair, respectful, and friendly? Imagine a world where every child grew up to become an adult who manifested those qualities. Can you imagine a

Washington, D.C., where every politician demonstrated these qualities? I can. I know Dorothy can. I am sure that is what motivates all of us who are in the business of "growing" people to continue our work.

Yours is a noble job—being a parent. Never underestimate the power you have in helping to create a better future, not only for your children but for everyone. This book can help you become the parent you have always wanted to be, raise the kind of children you can always be proud of, and contribute to the evolution of consciousness that will lead to the creation of the kind of world we all dream of living in.

The Story of "Children Learn What They Live"

I wrote "Children Learn What They Live" in 1954 as part of my weekly column on creative family living for a local newspaper in Southern California. At the time, I was the mother of a twelve-year-old daughter and a nine-year-old son. I taught family living in the adult education program of the local school district and served as director of parent education for a nursery school. I had no idea the poem was destined to become a world classic.

"Children Learn What They Live" was my way of responding to parents' questions in my family-life classes. The poem speaks to their concerns about what it means to be a parent. In the 1950s, parents raised their children by telling them what to do and what not to do. The concept of guiding your children was not widely known. "Children Learn What They Live" recognized that parents' greatest influence on their children is the example they set as role models in everyday living.

Over the years, "Children Learn What They Live" has appeared in many forums. Through Ross Products division of Abbott Laboratories, Inc., a shortened version of the poem has been and continues to be given to millions of new parents in hospitals and to physicians for their offices. The poem has been translated into ten languages and published worldwide, and is used internationally by teachers and clergy as part of the curriculum for parenting education and teacher-training classes. Wherever the poem appears, I hope it serves as a guide and inspiration to parents as they face the most important job of their lives—raising their children.

Changing Times

As the world has changed, I've made changes in the poem. The most significant structural change grew out of a greater sensitivity to gender issues. The poem was originally written "If a child lives with . . ., he learns. . . ." In the early eighties, I gave the poem more inclusive language: "If children live with . . . they learn . . ."

Around the same time I also separated one complex line, "If children live with honesty and fairness, they learn truth and justice," into two: "If children live with honesty, they learn truth" and "If children live with fairness, they learn justice." Children see honesty and fairness as separate qualities. The change also gave greater emphasis to truth and justice as distinct values. In 1990, I inserted a new line, "If children live with kindness and consideration, they learn respect." With the increasingly multicultural make-up of our society, I wanted to encourage the development of respect as the foundation for acceptance of differences among people.

While working on this book, I reflected once again on the line, "If children live with honesty, they learn truth." In the mid-fifties when I wrote the original poem, the concept of "truth" seemed very clear. However, more than four decades later, we've come to understand that there are many truths, and there are many shades of gray. So I've chosen to change the line to "If children live with honesty, they learn truthfulness." I think this conveys a more realistic expectation of children discovering their own truthfulness.

The poem as you see it printed in the front of this book is the complete, up-to-date "Children Learn What They Live."

Words Connect Us

Over the years, I've enjoyed a spontaneous intimacy with people who recognize me as the author of the poem. One mother told me, "You may not like this, but I keep your poem in the bathroom." This was the only place she had personal privacy. She retreated there when she felt she needed quiet time to remember to value herself as a parent. A father told me that he hung his copy of the poem over his workbench in the garage. "I read it when I've had it up to here," he said. In both these instances, "Children Learn What They Live" provided a way for parents to recognize when they need time out to restore themselves and regain their perspective.

A grandmother recently told me she refers to the poem for guidance in her relationship with her grandchildren. She said "Children Learn What They Live" was like her bible when raising her own children, and now she's using it with the next generation. Another mother wrote to tell me the poem "was my first parenting lesson." So many people have shared with me their personal relationship with "Children Learn What They Live" that I have come to understand that the poem can serve as an inspirational model for how they want to be as parents.

"Children Learn What They Live" presents a clear and simple message: Children are continuously learning from their parents. Your children are paying attention to you. Perhaps not to what you tell them to do, but certainly to what they actually see you do. You are their first and most powerful role models. Parents can strive to teach certain values, but children will inevitably absorb whatever values are transmitted through their parents' behavior, feelings, and attitudes in everyday living. How you express and manage your own feelings becomes a model that will be remembered by your children throughout their lifetimes.

I believe that each child is unique and has a center of creativity and wisdom that is his or hers alone. It is the privilege of parents to witness the unfolding of their child's inner self and allow its beauty to shine forth in the world.

I like to think "Children Learn What They Live" has withstood the test of time, providing a sensible approach to parenting for generations of families. It serves as a reminder that you can take the time to reconnect with what is important to you in your family life. I hope the poem and this book will guide and inspire you to trust your own feelings and intuition as you raise your children. Remember to appreciate and nurture your children's unique inner resources and their self-expression as they learn how to participate and contribute to family life. In this way, you can create a partnership with your children that will encourage and support growing, sharing, and learning together as a family.

When parents first read my poem, they often say, "I know that." It's true—you probably do. The poem is a connection to what you already know in your inner wisdom. My intention in this book is to expand the meaning in each couplet of "Children Learn What They Live." I like to imagine we're sitting down and talking together about living with children. I hope you feel that this is a sharing experience, and that my poem will become alive and real for you. Children *do* learn what they live. Then they grow up to live what they've learned.

—Dorothy Law Nolte

If children live with criticism, they learn to condemn

C hildren are like sponges. They soak up everything we do, everything we say. They're learning from us all the time, whether or not we realize we are teaching them. So if we fall into a pattern of being critical—of complaining about them, others, or the world around us—we are showing them how to condemn others, or perhaps even worse, to condemn themselves. We're teaching them to see what's wrong with the world, rather than what's right.

Criticism can be conveyed in dozens of ways—words, tone of voice, manner, or even a glance. We all know how to give a condemning look or add a critical edge to our words. Young children are especially sensitive to the way things are said and take them to heart. One parent can say, "Time to go" and mean nothing more than that. Another parent, who is rushed and impatient, can say the same words in a way that implies "You're bad for taking so long." Although neither way is guaranteed to be effective, the child will hear these two messages very differently, and the second one may leave him feeling bad about himself.

Of course, we all have our pet peeves and everyone criticizes now and then. We may even do so within earshot of our children. But this is not the same as living with a pervasive pattern of criticism, with its relentless focus on finding fault. Frequent criticism—regardless of where it's directed—has a cumulative effect, creating a negative, judgmental tone for family life. As parents, we have a choice—we can create an emotional atmosphere that is critical and condemning, or one that is supportive and encouraging.

In the Heat of the Moment

Six-year-old Abby is standing at the kitchen table arranging some flowers she picked in a plastic pitcher filled with water. Suddenly, the pitcher tips over, sending water, leaves, and flowers all over the place. Abby stands in the middle of it all, wet and wailing. Her mother is there in an instant.

"Oh no! How could you be so clumsy?" she says, in exasperation.

We've all said things like this. We react without thinking. The words fly out of our mouths so quickly that we surprise ourselves. Maybe we're tired. Maybe we're worried about something totally unrelated. However, it's not too late to change the tone, and prevent this minor mishap from being blown out of proportion and really damaging the child's sense of self worth. If Abby's mother stops herself, calms down, and apologizes for yelling, the cleanup will go better. Abby may feel bad about the incident, but not about herself. On the other hand, if Abby's mom continues to criticize, Abby may begin to see herself as an incompetent and clumsy person.

I know that reining in our feelings of annoyance, even when we know it's best for our children, is not always easy. Most of us have to work hard at understanding and taking charge of our own emotional reactions. It can help to have an alternative response ready, like, "How did it happen?" This puts the emphasis on the event instead of the child. Not only does this spare the child feelings of inadequacy and failure, but it makes room for constructive learning. By encouraging the child to talk through the sequence of events, together you can see how one thing led to another and maybe even discover what you could do differently in the future.

Some accidents can be prevented by taking more time to plan and by setting boundaries at the beginning of a project. For the most part, our kids want to please us, and we can make it easier for them to do so by saying clearly what we want at the outset. Our suggestions need to be specific and age-appropriate, and they need to be said in a way that offers the child concrete information he can use to guide his behavior.

One rainy day, four-year-old Ben told his mom that he

and his friend wanted to make animals out of play dough. His mother was in the middle of paying bills, and was tempted to simply say okay, and leave the boys to their own devices. Instead, she got up and pulled out an old shower curtain she had saved for this purpose. Spreading it over the floor, she explained to the boys, "Sit in the middle here, and we can straighten it all the way out. There'll be plenty of room for your animal farm."

While the boys were piling the play dough onto the plastic, Ben asked his mom, "Can we use some knives from the kitchen?"

"No knives. Knives are not for play. How about some cookie cutters?" she responded.

"Okay. And some wooden spoons?" Ben countered.

"Sure," his mom said, getting out an assortment of kitchen utensils. "And remember, you guys get to help with the cleanup too."

The few minutes invested at the beginning of the project were an interruption for Ben's mom, but they may well have saved her from finding herself scraping play dough out of the carpet later while trying not to criticize both children. Her early involvement also gave Ben a chance to negotiate for the kitchen things he wanted to play with. Although this approach takes time, it allows choices to emerge and provides children with good practice in decision making. Having an active voice in everyday decisions also helps them to build a positive self-image as a competent person.

Realistically, we don't always have the time or the foresight to handle things as carefully as we'd like. One day a friend of mine was rushing her five-year-old daughter, Katie, out of the house to do a bunch of errands, including getting Katie's hair trimmed. On the way, she said, "Hurry up, sweetie. We're getting your hair cut and I don't want to be late." Suddenly, out of the blue, Katie pitched a fit about getting a haircut. Frustrated, her mom told her she was "willful," whereupon Katie got so upset she literally couldn't talk. To an adult, it may not seem like Katie's mom was being critical, but the message Katie heard was, "You're bad because you're willful."

When Katie finally calmed down, she was able to explain that she wanted to grow her bangs out and didn't want them cut. Her mother, upon realizing that this was what the big fuss was about, stared at her in disbelief. "Okay, honey," she said, "we'll just explain that to the hairdresser. We won't let him cut your bangs." If she had thought to discuss the haircut with Katie over breakfast, she could probably have saved both Katie and herself the ordeal of going through a tantrum.

Of course, no matter how flexible and patient we are or how much we can anticipate things in advance, there will always be times when we disagree with our children. The issue then is how to resolve the conflict with minimal damage. Nobody wins in a stalemate. Katie's mom respected her daughter's right to decide how she wanted her hair cut. This sharing of control over small issues builds trust for future negotiations over bigger decisions as children become teenagers. If our kids grow up knowing that we will listen to them and respectfully consider their ideas, they will be more willing to talk to us and work together to resolve problems.

The Way We Say Things

Often when we criticize our children our purpose is to encourage them to do better, to be better. Perhaps this is how our own parents communicated with us when we were kids. Or perhaps we revert to criticizing them when we're stressed or tired. But children don't experience criticism as encouraging. To a child, criticism feels more like a personal attack and it is more likely to make him defensive than cooperative. And young children may find it difficult to understand that it's their behavior that is unacceptable, not themselves.

However, we can still tell our children we don't like what they're doing. If we take the time to consider the impact of our words, we can say what we need to without diminishing the child's sense of self. No matter what has happened, we can let him know that *he* is okay, even if what he did was not.

As soon as William's dad heard the crash, he knew exactly what had happened. He walked calmly from the kitchen to the living room window, where broken glass lay shattered on the floor. His eight-year-old son stood outside with a look of astonishment and fear on his face. The baseball bat was lying on the ground nearby, the ball on the living room floor.

"Now do you know why the rule is, 'Never play baseball close to the house?'" his father asked.

William looked down. "I know, Dad. I was being careful."

"No, Will, the rule is not about being careful." Dad was firm. "The rule is about distance."

"I'm sorry," William said, hoping that would end the discussion.

Dad looked at him seriously. "Well, let's find out what it'll cost to repair the window, and then we can figure out how long it'll take you to save your allowance to pay for it."

The words sunk in slowly as William realized the consequences of his mistake. Dad watched his son's shoulders slump with the weight of the responsibility.

"You know, Grandpa made me pay for a window I broke when I was about your age," he confessed to his son, who was now listening with rapt attention.

"Really?"

"It took a long time, too." Dad said. "And I'll tell you, I never broke another window after that. Now run get a brush and dustpan, and we'll get rid of this glass"

Too much emphasis on blame or punishment creates separation, not togetherness. The truth is, we all make mistakes, and accidents happen. Responding with helpful messages at these times makes it easier for our children to learn through experience, to make the connection between what they have done and what "happened," and to determine what they may need to do to set things right again.

Nag, Nag, Nag

We may not realize it, but chronic nagging and complaining are subtle forms of criticism. The message underlying nagging is, "I don't trust you to remember to do something or to behave appropriately." Expecting the worst from our children is neither helpful to them nor productive to us. Even very young children quickly learn to tune out oft-repeated phrases, and teenagers are famous for their ability to "turn deaf" with or without earphones in place.

A better strategy than nagging is to set up predictable routines with reasonable expectations. For example, I often suggest to parents that one simple but effective way to get around the "don't forget" habit is to stop emphasizing forgetting and start emphasizing remembering. Tell your child what you want her to remember. "Remember to put your socks in the laundry hamper" and "Remember, this doll stays indoors." This sets an encouraging tone which is important at any age and can make all the difference in the world. It is particularly helpful for the young child who is just learning how family life works. Above all, give them credit for their accomplishments. "What a good helper you are to remember to put your blocks away!" With positive remarks such as these, you are letting your child know what you expect and you're also encouraging her.

Like nagging, complaining is an ineffective way to seek change and not a beneficial model to teach our children. Complaining focuses on difficulties, deficiencies, and disappointments, not solutions. We don't want our children to learn to see the world with this passive, negative perspective, or to think that the way to respond to problems is to complain about them. Avoid making complaining a substitute for taking action, and instead try to dream up as many creative solutions as possible, and get the kids to come up with some, too.

Think about how much complaining you do in your everyday life: It may be surprising to realize how much we really do complain, whether about our work situation, other people in our lives, or even the weather. Although we may all need to grouse once in a while, remember that those "No Whining" buttons apply to parents, too.

Complaining about our spouses is especially destructive. It can make children feel they need to side with one parent over the other, placing them in the middle of a marital struggle. This is an impossible position for children, as they feel torn between their loyalties for both parents. In a similar way, complaining about our children's grandparents also places our kids in an untenable spot. Our complaints about our parents or in-laws need to be discussed privately and kept separate from our children's magical relationship with their grandparents. Our kids will soon enough discover our family's faults. Let's not burden them with our gripes prematurely. Plus, children need to see all the adults in their family treating each other with respect in both words and deeds. Observing our interactions is how children learn about relationships and how loved ones get along together.

Enjoying Your Child's Glow

Just as our children are continually learning from us, we can continually learn from them. After a family night out, some friends of mine were focused on getting their seven- and eight-year-old sons out of the car and into bed with as little fuss as possible. Neither boy wanted to go to bed, as usual. As they were walking toward the house, the younger son asked, "Can't we just watch the stars for a little bit?"

The parents stopped. They had a choice. They could have said, "You love to stall. Don't be so difficult. It's late, it's time for bed." But they didn't. That night, they took a few minutes to enjoy the night sky and the reflected glow in their children's faces.

"Watching the stars" is qualitatively different from "looking at the stars." Adults look, see, and quickly move on to what "has to" be done. Children watch the stars with wonder and anticipation. Allowing our children to teach us new ways of seeing the world creates a dynamic family experience in which we can all learn and grow together.

If children live with hostility, they learn to fight

Most of us don't think of ourselves as hostile. We know we're not like the violent, abusive families who make the headlines on the local news. Yet we may still be creating an atmosphere of unrecognized resentment in the home with unexpressed anger that may leak into the family dynamic and can erupt unexpectedly.

Certainly our culture offers plenty of examples of hostility and fighting. At any point in time, war is being waged somewhere on the planet. In our own country, hate crimes, domestic abuse, gang warfare, and the like are a part of our everyday awareness. Children are exposed to thousands of hours of images of fighting and violence through TV and movies. Hostility can explode, even on a daily basis for some children, between siblings at home, classmates at school, and between strangers on the street, behind the wheel, or in the neighborhood. Kids may also see or hear about their parents fighting with each other, their bosses, or the neighbors.

Living in an atmosphere of hostility makes children

feel vulnerable. Some children react by becoming tough, with a chip on their shoulder, always ready to respond to trouble or even go looking for it. Others become so frightened of fighting that they avoid any kind of conflict, even mild confrontations. These roles are played out on every elementary school playground.

A pattern of aggression in the family can teach children that fighting is a necessity, a solution of sorts. Children may grow up expecting that life will be a battle, that they won't be treated fairly without a fight, or that they have to fight to survive. This is not what we want for our children. How we, as parents, resolve our differences and handle family crises sets the stage for our children to learn how to deal with conflicts—either with destructive hostility and fighting or constructive dialogue and resolution.

Storm Clouds Building

Usually it's the everyday, little things that drive us crazy. Our frustrations build and sometimes our tempers flare, not necessarily over a significant event, but over whatever is "the last straw." We lose our equanimity as stress builds, often when the family is reuniting, tired and hungry, at the end of a long day.

Four-year-old Frank has had a rough day at preschool. He didn't get a turn at the computer and he felt his teacher didn't make the other kids share enough. Then Dad was late picking him up due to an emergency in the office.

On their way home, Dad asks, "How was school?" pretending to be chipper and interested, when really he's tired, harried, and preoccupied.

"Fine," Frank answers directly from the back seat of the car, staring vacantly out the window. The radio is tuned to the news. Traffic is slow.

When they arrive home, Mom is rushing around the kitchen trying to put dinner together. A fast-paced news magazine is playing on the small TV on the counter. Everyone is hungry. As he is taking off his jacket, Frank accidentally knocks his lunch box off the counter, scattering cracker crumbs all over the floor.

This scene probably sounds familiar, and it's easy to imagine what might happen next. Many of us live similarly hectic lives and know how difficult it is to juggle everything that is demanded of us. How well we respond to the stress depends upon our ability to handle our feelings of impatience, dissatisfaction, annoyance, and irritation at tense moments. These "smaller" feelings need to be acknowledged and dealt with in a creative way as they arise or else they build over time, and turn into "big" feelings—first smoldering resentment then out-and-out anger which can erupt at critical moments. Fortunately, in this case, Mom is able to handle her initial annoyance and manage the situation well.

She hands Frank a small dustpan and brush, saying, "That's okay, honey. Here, you can use this to clean it up."

Then, after getting the chicken in the oven, she kneels down next to him and says encouragingly, "You got almost all of them. Here, let me help you get the rest of the crumbs." She takes the brush and sweeps the remaining bits into the dustpan Frank is still holding. His face relaxes into a grateful smile.

We all know this scene could easily have had a different outcome. After dropping his lunch box, Frank could have exploded in frustration and shouted, "I hate this lunch box! I hate school!" Mom could have blamed Dad for the accident, yelling "How can you just walk in and leave Frank with me while I'm cooking?" or criticized Frank, complaining, "Another mess! Can't you be more careful?"

It's far better to address our feelings of frustration, even if only to ourselves, when they come up, because children learn how to deal with the feelings that escalate from impatience to hostility to outright fighting by observing how we handle them ourselves. Interestingly, we might be able to learn ways of releasing tensions from our young kids. When children spontaneously stop what they're doing and turn to an activity that expends energy—like running, drawing, or role-playing with dolls—they are often instinctively discharging frustration. Instead of losing our tempers, we can try dispelling our anger by doing something physical—going for a quick walk, digging in the garden, or even washing the car. If we don't have time for a change of activity, we can simply focus on our breathing, taking a few deep breaths and slowly counting to ten, like our grandmothers used to do. The goal is to let go of tension and return to feeling more in charge. Not only will this help us through the tense moment, it sets a good example for our children.

For those times when kids don't dispel their tensions naturally, through play, we can teach them how to deal with their feelings using an imagination game. After his rough day at preschool, Frank's mom or dad could have asked him, "What kind of animal did you feel like at school today?" He might have answered, "I felt like going 'grrr' like a lion." They could have followed up by asking him what kind of animal he felt like now that he was home, and he might well have answered, "Right now I feel like a cuddly puppy." Such an answer would let his parents know that he needed some hugging and nurturing after a hard day.

Dealing With Dark Clouds

Children have an inherent right to acknowledge and express their feelings, including angry feelings, just as we do. This does not mean that they have the right to disrupt or harm others or to damage property. Certain behaviors, including hitting, kicking, biting, and shoving, should not be tolerated, and should result in disciplinary action, such as a time out. Young children especially need our help learning to express their feelings in words rather than by putting them into action. As parents, we need to accept and respect our children's feelings of frustration, while maintaining rules and limits of behavior. Finding a consistent balance can be a challenge.

During the afternoon, Mom interrupts some bickering between her nine-year-old daughter, Tessa, and a visiting girlfriend. "It's not nice to get angry at your friend," she says. "Now, both of you, stop it."

Later on, Mom yells at Tessa for not brushing her teeth. Tessa responds by saying, "It's not nice to get angry at your daughter." Mom goes ballistic.

If Mom can stop for a moment and take a deep breath, she'll realize that Tessa is not mocking her or trying to undermine her authority. She is just confronting her mother with the inconsistency of her message. Tessa is questioning the premise that grown-ups can get angry, but children can't; or that people can get angry at her, but she can't get angry at them. She is right to question: this double standard is not what we want to teach our children.

I suggest that parents allow their children to define their feelings themselves. One way of helping them to do this is to replace statements with questions. Instead of saying, "I know you're angry about . . ." try "What bothers you about . . . ?" or "What's upsetting you about . . . ?" Then follow up with "What might make you feel better about it?" This helps children sort out their feelings and discover a wider range of ways to deal with them.

Our Own Dark Clouds

How we handle our own feelings of impatience, hostility, and anger is a far more powerful example to our children than what we tell them to do with theirs. We don't want to impose our black moods on our children, but neither do we want to pretend that our angry feelings don't exist. In any case, we may as well be honest, for even when we try to cover up our anger, our children sense how we feel.

Sam's mother was busily straightening up the house one Saturday morning after a tough week at work. Noticing that she was throwing the couch pillows around with an extra vengeance, the nine-year-old asked her, "Are you mad at me?"

Mom stopped, gathered herself together and said, "No, sweetie, of course not."

So Sam went outside to play, confused and unsettled, but not sure what to do about it. His mom could have said, more honestly, "Yes, I am upset. I wish you wouldn't leave your toys in the living room. It's enough work for me to keep it clean without having to first cart all your stuff to your room. Would you please help me by taking these games out of here?" This way, Sam would know that his perception was accurate, that Mom was angry. He would also know exactly what she expected of him.

Children also need to learn that parents can get mad at each other and still resolve their differences. Seven-year-old Carla woke up around midnight one night and heard her parents' angry voices. She was scared and hid under the covers, finally going back to sleep. The next morning, realizing that Carla had heard their argument, Dad explained to her "Mom and I were discussing our budget and we had a disagreement. I'm sorry we woke you up."

It's important for Carla to know that her parents had indeed been arguing, but that things were still okay. Dad could further explain, "Your mom and I disagreed, but we think we found a compromise. If that doesn't work, then we'll find another way." This kind of reassurance would help Carla understand that everybody gets upset and fights sometimes, but that it doesn't mean they don't love each other. She would also learn that not every decision is arrived at easily, that some involve disagreements and that more than one attempt at resolution may be required. By being honest with our children about the inevitable difficulties encountered in living together with others, we can turn a potentially upsetting incident into an opportunity for teaching valuable lessons about the important life skills of compromise and negotiation, lessons they will be able to use both now and in the future.

Sunny With Intermittent Clouds

For most of us, feelings of hostility come and go like cloudy weather. Like the weather, it's easy to think of frustration as something that "happens" to us, that we don't have a lot of control over. As we come to understand our reactions, we can begin to see how we help make them happen. The more creatively and constructively we can handle our anger, the less likely our hostile feelings will lead to fighting. For fighting only seems to lead to more fighting.

The irony about dealing with these intense feelings is that we are more likely to get angry with loved ones in the family than acquaintances, friends, or strangers. This is why it is so important to deal with these feelings as they arise, before they can gain momentum. Annoyance is much easier to deal with than full-fledged anger.

It's important and reassuring to know that we don't have to be perfect role models for our children. There will inevitably be times when we lose our tempers. If we are able to acknowledge and evaluate our mistakes and apologize for our behavior, our children will learn an important lesson—that Mom and Dad are continually learning better ways of dealing with their feelings, too. It's important to demonstrate to our children that anger is not an enemy to resist, but an energy to take charge of creatively. What we do with that energy and how we direct it is important for ourselves and our whole family's health and well-being. After all, it is our everyday behaviors that create the family patterns that our children will pass on to their future families—our grandchildren.

If children live with fear, they learn to be apprehensive

C hildren love to play with the notion of fear. They delight in bogeyman games and are thrilled by scary stories and horror movies. I remember when I was a preteen, I used to spend every Friday night at one or another friend's house, huddled around the radio with the lights turned off. We listened to a show called *The Witches Tales,* which would probably sound very tame today, but terrified us. The hardest (and also the most thrilling) part was trying to act unafraid when we were walking home in the dark after the show. We experienced the adrenaline rush of heart-pounding fear wondering what lurked in the shadows, while knowing deep inside that we were perfectly safe and would soon arrive home to our cosy, well-lit houses.

Living with real fear is quite a different story, whether it's a threat of physical violence, psychological abuse, abandonment, catastrophic illness, or the seemingly smaller fear of the neighborhood bully or monsters under the bed. Living with real fear day to day tears down a child's self-confidence and basic sense of security. Fear undermines the supportive environment a child needs to grow, explore, and learn, leaving him with a persistent feeling of apprehension, a general anxiety that can fundamentally damage his way of relating to people and facing new situations.

Things That Go Bump in the Night

Many of the sources of real fear in children's lives can come as a total surprise to their parents. Children can be genuinely frightened by things adults take in stride, whether it's a new dog in the neighborhood or that old maple tree with the dead branches. They can even be frightened by casual turns of phrase. A three-year-old I know asked her mother, "Mommy, are you really going to fall apart? You said so to Aunt Cathy." Sometimes a young child takes a figure of speech quite literally. This little girl needed her mom to explain what she meant, along with some reassurance and a warm hug.

No matter what the reason, if your child is afraid, the situation needs to be taken seriously. Fear is in the eye of the beholder, and we need to see the world from our child's perspective. Saying things like, "Don't be silly," "That's nothing," "Grow up," "Don't be a sissy," only belittles the child, driving her fears underground where they continue to grow.

In my parenting groups, participants often ask me, "How do you know the difference between a fearful child and one who just wants attention?" The answer is, you don't. Parents shouldn't be overly concerned with being manipulated by their child's emotional needs. Your child's need for attention is as legitimate as her need for food and shelter. And sometimes a child is both frightened *and* needs attention.

Three-year-old Adam provides a good example. His family had recently moved into a new house, he had started preschool, and his baby sister had just been born. Now these were all happy developments for his parents, but for Adam, they marked the end of life as he knew it. He felt his world was in complete upheaval. One night, when his mother was out, Adam came to his dad with an unusual request.

"I'm scared. Protect me," he cried.

His father might have said, "Protect you? From what? You're a big brother now and you shouldn't be afraid," and sent Adam back to bed alone.

Instead, his dad understood. "Protect you? Sure, no problem," he responded. "Come snuggle next to me, and we'll be safe together." His understanding words and the physical closeness gave Adam the reassurance he needed to get through a tough moment and move on.

Parents can magically dispel even older children's fears. Two brothers, ages six and eight, would periodically get spooked about ghosts in the attic. Their mother kept an old broom in her clothes closet for just these occasions.

When the boys would tear into her room, wide-eyed and scared, she would calmly take the broom from the closet and run through the house wielding it like a dangerous weapon, screaming at the top of her lungs. The boys would run behind her, laughing with glee and the certainty that she was chasing every possible scary creature out of the house.

When Magic Won't Work

Of course, there are times when there is no magical way to protect our children from their fears. Neither a broom-wielding mom nor a cozy hug will banish the fear or sadness that comes when a family hits a real crisis. The worst times for kids are when the structure or daily routines of the family are fundamentally disrupted. Kids rely on the rhythms of family life remaining more or less consistent, and when a crisis occurs, it can feel to them as if their world is falling apart.

Aside from the death of a parent, divorce is probably the most frightening event in a child's life. Many children live with the fear of divorce, whether or not the fear is a realistic one. Hearing one parent complain about the other increases this fear, creating anxiety in the child. Underlying the fear of divorce is the child's fear of abandonment. The child believes that if one of their parents leaves the house, they're leaving her, too.

During a divorce, children feel like they have lost control over their world. One of the biggest challenges for divorcing parents is to choose to act in the best interests of their children, no matter how hurt, frustrated, and angry they are with each other. Children are inevitably caught in the middle, so it's up to the parents to declare a truce when it comes to the kids. This is far easier said than done, especially when parents are angry and quarreling with each other. But this is also the time when your children need the most reassurance that no matter what else happens, you are both still their parents, and together you will take care of them.

Any family crisis is felt by the children even though they may not fully understand the implications. Overhearing that her father might lose his job, six-year-old Lynne became frightened that her family would become homeless and hungry. Dad explained to her, "We'll find a way to get along. We may have to cut back on some of our spending for a while, but we'll make it." This gave Lynne the opportunity to be courageous and do her part for the family. "I don't really need those new sneakers, not yet anyway," she said.

Our Fears for Our Children

Children absorb parental worries, often without our even knowing it. It's worth becoming aware of how often we make statements beginning with the words "I'm afraid . . ." or "Maybe it won't . . ." or "I'm worried that . . ." If children are routinely exposed to fearful comments, they are likely to develop an apprehensive mind-set. Expectations are molded through repetition, and negative thinking can quickly become circular. We all know people who have become caught in this kind of negative spiral "I expect the worst, and the worst always seems to happen to me."

Unfortunately, today's parents have more serious fears for their children than ever before. We face the dilemma of figuring out how to protect and warn our children against danger without instilling unnecessary anxiety in them. For example, we want our children to be cautious with strangers but not to assume that every person they don't know is hostile or out to do them harm. We want them to stay in our eyesight, but not to feel vulnerable if we aren't by their side. It's a challenge to raise self-confident kids and at the same time do our best to keep them out of harm's way.

There are no easy answers to this dilemma, and parents must individually weigh how to answer their kids' questions, how much independence to give them, and at what age. When four-year-old Allison asked if it was okay to go to the park, and since there would be strangers there, her mom answered calmly, "Yes, Allison. I'll be there with you and I'll be watching out for you." When ten-year-old Ken announced that he wanted to walk to school alone, his parents had to balance their anxiety over his being alone on city streets with their desire to encourage his budding independence.

Another fear we have as parents is that our children will suffer like we did when we were their age. Our over-identification with our children may lead us to behave in inappropriate ways. Carl's dad is a zealot about T-ball, driving everyone crazy with his obsession—from his wife to the coach to his seven-year-old son. The father explained his concerns to me this way. "I wasn't very athletic when I was Carl's age. I remember being the last kid picked to be on a team, and I was miserable. I'm afraid the same thing will happen to Carl."

Carl needs to be allowed to explore his own athletic abilities without the burden of his dad's memories. In short, Dad has to back off and give his son the chance to have his own experiences. We have to remember that our children are different from us, and that they have the right to suffer their own sorrows.

Everyday Fears

Children live in a different world than adults, and they don't always tell us what's going on in theirs. It's easy for parents to be unaware of the things that frighten their kids on a daily basis. For example, many children live with daily intimidation by other kids at school, in the neighborhood, or even by siblings at home. They may be bullied, threatened, called names, or teased. Younger kids may not know how to express their fear and hurt, and older kids may feel they ought to be able to handle things by themselves. We need to take the time to ask our children how they're getting along with the other kids in their lives.

Mom casually asks Andrew, her five-year-old son, "What happened in school today?" (This phrasing tends to yield more information than the more loaded, "How was school today?")

"Joey took my truck. I was playing with it first."

"Then what happened?"

Andrew looks down and mutters, "Nothing. I don't know."

At this point, Mom realizes that Joey is intimidating her son and tries to help Andrew figure out a way to deal with a bully. "I imagine it was very frustrating having Joey take your truck. What do you think could you have done about it?" she asks him, providing him with the opportunity to think of new ways of handling a difficult situation.

Andrew talks about grabbing the truck back, telling the teacher, playing with something else, moving away from Joey, and joining other kids. Mom doesn't even need to tell Andrew what he *should* do. She only needs to listen and help Andrew explore various alternatives to "nothing." It can also be helpful to ask, "How do you wish this could have turned out?"

Andrew might answer, "I wish I had the truck."

Once a child has clarified what he wants, he can begin to develop a constructive plan. "I think I'll get the truck first tomorrow morning, and if Joey tries to take it, I'll tell him, 'No!'"

For many young kids, facing new situations is scary. The first day of school, the first visit to the dentist, the first airplane trip can all be overwhelming. We can help our children through these milestones by being generous with our support and encouragement. Expressing our confidence in our children is a powerful way to teach them to be confident in themselves. Notice the physical reaction in your child's face and posture the next time you say, "You'll do fine. I know you can handle it."

Very young children may need extra preparation for first-time situations, like going to visit the new preschool classroom before school begins. After she had explored all the different learning areas of the classroom, a mom I know asked her daughter, "What do you think you'll want to do first?"

"Feed the fish," Sandy replied without hesitation, already having taken the big step of imagining herself in school.

Another source of fear for some kids is television, with its daily menu of violence in the news, films, advertising, and dramatic programming. Young children may not be able to distinguish between reality and fiction, and need to be protected from both. Some older kids can watch the accidents, trauma, violence, and murder that TV offers up and take it in stride, while other children become upset and obsessed with the images. We each need to evaluate our own children's ability to handle TV violence and limit their viewing accordingly.

Everyone's Afraid . . . Sometimes

As parents, we want to be strong for our kids. We want them to feel that they can rely on us to keep them safe. But we also need to have the courage to be vulnerable and share those moments when we feel like the Cowardly Lion in *The Wizard of Oz*. We're all afraid now and again. It's how we deal with our fear that makes the difference. This helps our children learn that we're human, that part of being human is being imperfect, and that we all need support or reassurance at times. It can be amazingly comforting to feel a small hand patting us on the back in the middle of a hug.

Eight-year-old Phoebe knew her mom was worried about her doctor's appointment that day. Phoebe didn't know all the details and she didn't need to; they would have been too much for her to understand. But that morning, when Mom leaned over to hug her goodbye before school, Phoebe was the one to give her mom a reassuring squeeze. Mom felt the difference in her embrace and with a surprised look on her face said, "Thanks, Phoebe. That helps."

Our children learn how to deal with their fears by observing how we deal with ours. Let them see the small and large ways we seek support from our spouse, friends, and family when we need it, and how at other times, we offer support and reassurance to them in return. How we acknowledge our feelings and find creative solutions during our difficult times is the model our children will have to follow when they face their own crises.

If children live with pity, they learn to feel sorry for themselves

Feeling sorry for yourself is a lot like getting caught in quicksand. In both cases a mysterious force pulls you down until you're feeling overwhelmed and helpless. Your only hope is that someone will come along and rescue you.

This is not a recipe for success. If we feel pity toward our children or are filled with self-pity ourselves, we are teaching them that it's okay to feel sorry for themselves. This doesn't teach them initiative, perseverance, or enthusiasm. On the contrary, feeling sorry for oneself is de-energizing and often projects an image of helplessness and inadequacy.

We want our kids to be resourceful, to be able to find within themselves the strength they need, and to be able to ask for help from others when they need it. To set a good example for them, we need to be able to do this in our own lives. Maybe not perfectly and maybe not all the time, but enough so that our children learn to tap their inner strengths for the challenges they encounter. This means that we have to find the strength within ourselves to face the challenges life presents us head-on. We also have to have faith in our children, believing that they will rise to the occasion when they encounter obstacles in their own lives.

Trying on a Different Hat

We all have moments when we feel sorry for ourselves. We feel overworked, underappreciated, like life isn't going our way. "Why me?" we may ask ourselves. If we aren't careful, self-pity can become a state of mind, leading from occasional moping to full-blown hopelessness. Our perception narrows to take in only the information that supports the "poor-me" outlook, and we get caught up in repetitive, circular thinking that leads into a vicious cycle of self-pity and helplessness.

If we find ourselves in such a situation, it can be helpful to stop thinking about our problems and try doing something—anything! I advise parents to get on an exercise bike, take a brisk walk, or simply imagine a trip to a favorite place. One of my students, Kate, told me what worked for her. "I was feeling like an old dishrag, used and unappreciated," she said. "My three kids were running me ragged, my husband was working all the time and was exhausted when he got home. I was feeling angry and blue, but I was also sick of feeling that way. So I decided to try some imaging, as we had discussed in class. I closed my eyes and the first thing I came up with was that I needed some applause. So I pictured myself standing in a huge stadium filled with people clapping and shouting 'Kate is Great!' Then *I* started clapping. I was reminded of an old rhyme—'Two, four, six, eight, who do we appreciate? Kate!' I yelled to the kitchen walls.

"I realized I needed to be closer to my husband and that I wanted the kids to notice what I did for them. I wanted some attention. So I baked everybody's favorite dessert, and put it on the sideboard with a big sign that said 'Kate is great. If you agree, give me a big hug.' Needless to say, this sparked some conversation. I got the hugs I needed, and my husband and I made plans to leave the kids with my aunt and spend some time together the next weekend. I'm not saying it changed my life, but it got me out of my poor-me rut."

Not only did Kate benefit from her resourcefulness, but she showed her kids how to take creative action to address a problem. Plus, she gained needed time with her husband. It is important for husband and wife to enrich and revitalize their relationship. Everyone in the family benefits from their greater appreciation of each other.

You Don't Know How Lucky You Are

One of the most common themes for a parent stuck in a poor-me pattern involves making comparisons between the child's life and the parent's memories of her own childhood. Eleven-year-old Judith always knew when her mother was headed in this direction because she would begin to talk about what her life had been like at Judith's age, move on to how lucky Judith was to have so much, and how she didn't realize how hard her parents worked. The conversation usually took place in the car, where Judith had no escape.

Judith's mom would often start with comments like, "Kids today take things for granted, like hundred-dollar sneakers."

Judith couldn't think of what to say, other than a mumbled "Uh huh," slumping in her seat. But Mom was just warming up.

"I don't think you realize that when I was your age, I had a job baby-sitting three nights a week and Saturday afternoons. I didn't run around with my friends all the time."

At this point, Judith would roll her eyes and sigh, but she couldn't maintain her patience. "Mom, I don't run around with my friends all the time. And I do a lot of homework." Pause. "Probably more than you ever did."

This situation has created a contest between mother and daughter over who has more right to feel sorry for herself. Mom didn't mean to start this competition, or even to express self-pity. Her intent was to teach Judith to be more appreciative and grateful for what she has. But her underlying message comes across as, "I'm jealous and disappointed that I didn't have the advantages you do" along with the more subtle, and insidious, "You owe me." It's no wonder Judith starts sighing every time her mother starts this routine.

There's nothing wrong with directly expressing our need for appreciation. When picking her up at school, Judith's mom could simply say, "I'm glad I'm able to do this for you, and it would make me even happier to know you appreciate it." She doesn't have to fall into self-pity in order to make a clear request for appreciation. Of course, we can't guarantee how our kids will respond, but we're more likely to get what we want from them if our messages are clear, direct, and free of "old baggage."

"My Tummy Hurts"

Children can be masters at feeling sorry for themselves, and at eliciting parental pity and all its auxiliary advantages—being noticed, held, and soothed.

"My tummy hurts," four-year-old Tracy moans as her mother tries to get her ready for nursery school. "I don't wanna go." She's holding her stomach mournfully.

No parent escapes this dilemma. Is Tracy really sick? Should she stay home from school? Does she need to see her pediatrician? Is she avoiding something or someone at school? Does she need more attention from her parents? Or does she just need a day off to be quietly at home with Mom or Dad?

Tracy's mom will have to evaluate this particular situation and make her best guess. What's most important is that Tracy doesn't learn that acting pitiful will help her to get her needs met.

If Mom suspects that the stomachache is an excuse to avoid going to school, she could ask Tracy questions like, "What's the worst thing that could happen if you do go to school today?" "If you had the day off, what would you like to do?" "How would you like this day to turn out?" or "What can you do to help make it that way?"

Answering these questions could help Tracy identify what she really needs and wants for herself, without encouraging a "poor-me" attitude. It might also give Mom a window into Tracy's life. Sometimes when kids pretend to be sick it's a cry for attention. We might ask ourselves if we have been especially rushed or preoccupied lately. We may need to slow down, take stock, and spend some extra time with our children.

Another way kids may indulge in self-pity is by saying, "I can't." This can be the ultimate excuse and defense against developing new skills. The child is saying to the parent, "You can't possibly expect me to do what you want. I'm just not capable." However what she may really mean is, "I don't want to" or even more forcefully, "I won't."

If we fall for this strategy we are basically agreeing with our child's assertion that she is not capable. We don't want to give her this message. Even though it may be difficult, there are times we need to challenge our children, ignoring their excuses and maintaining our positive expectations of them. At the same time, we'd do well to help them define and acknowledge their feelings of insecurity.

Eight-year-old Ben was frustrated with his math homework. "I can't do this," he whined. "It's too hard for me."

Ben's dad took his frustration seriously, but ignored his bid for pity and encouraged him to keep trying. "Remember last year, when you had trouble with math?" he replied. "You asked your teacher for extra help, and we worked on some of the problems together. You got through it then, and you can get through it now. Let's take another look at it."

It's tempting to provide sympathy when our children are feeling discouraged, but it may only encourage them to wallow in self-pity just when they need to be developing the quality of perseverance. If his dad had responded by saying, "Okay, Ben, I know it's hard. Why not take a break for the night?" it might have started Ben on the path of thinking he just wasn't good at math. We want to encourage our children to keep their horizons open by helping them to achieve competency in a wide variety of disciplines and activities. It is particularly important to not let our own shortcomings cloud our perspective in this area. If Ben's dad has trouble with math himself, he might be tempted to "go easy" on Ben. But this would not be in Ben's best interest.

It can be very difficult for parents to know when to help their child and when not to. At times, helping can actually be a hindrance. Sometimes children need to complete projects on their own in order to develop confidence. At other times, not helping them can be hurtful. When a child is floundering and feeling overwhelmed, a parent may need to step in, helping in such a way that the child's confidence is bolstered, not undermined. Sometimes the best thing to do is to help the child get started on a project and then let go, encouraging her to find her own way.

As parents, the decisions about how, when, and whether to offer or withhold help must be constantly reassessed. Our kids' needs and abilities change as they mature—what is helpful to a three-year-old may be a hindrance to a five-year-old. We must learn to be good at gauging when to step in and when to step aside, all the while offering encouragement. It is important to remember that a certain amount of struggle is inevitable and can even be helpful to the learning process.

The Worst of Times

E ven when tragedy strikes, pity doesn't help. That's because pity is a distancing emotion. We feel sorry for the victim, yet at the same time grateful, and perhaps even a bit superior, because we've been spared. Empathy, on the other hand, is a feeling of closeness, of trying to imagine how it would feel to be in another person's shoes. It involves compassion, and leads naturally to asking ourselves how we can help.

One of the extraordinary things about tragedy is the way it can bring out the best in people. Victims of bad fortune often rise to the occasion with amazing strength and courage. Disabled children, for example, frequently teach their parents more about how to live than their parents can ever teach them. Even children with terminal illnesses are often able to rise above feeling sorry for themselves. They may feel discouraged at times, but they don't get stuck there.

Ten-year-old Sue had terminal cancer. She shuttled frequently between her fifth-grade classroom and the children's cancer ward at the hospital. All of her long, blond hair fell out. She could have spent her time hiding out and feeling sorry for herself. Instead, with her family's help, she maintained a normal ten-year-old's life as long as possible. She tied a scarf around her head and continued going to school, doing homework, and seeing her friends. While she still had the energy to enjoy it, she threw a party for her entire class. The children had a wonderful time, and so did Sue.

If her classmates had been consumed with pity for Sue, they would not have been able to play such a rousing game of tag, chasing after her with the same vigor as they do with everyone else. It's not that these kids weren't aware of Sue's illness, and they didn't lack sympathy for her. They had talked about the situation with their teacher and tried to imagine how Sue must be feeling. Because they had discussed her illness openly, and were able to understand the implications of it, they were able to be supportive, and to include her in their activities rather than shutting her out in a misguided attempt to protect her.

Solutions, Not Sympathy

Ten-year-old Janice flops onto the living room sofa next to Mom and complains, "I'm the only one not invited to Melissa's party."

Mom knows immediately where this conversation is heading. She puts her arm around Janice's slumped shoulders and inquires, "The *only* one not invited?"

"Well," Janice admits, "a few other kids aren't going."

"What would you like to do that night?" Mom asks.

"I could hang around the house and mope," Janice answers, partly serious, but looking at her mother sideways, with some interest.

"That's one option," Mom replies, not falling into the trap of feeling sorry for her daughter.

"Could I have a sleep-over with the other girls who aren't going?" Janice asks.

"That sounds like fun," Mom answers. "You can bake those brownies you like, too."

We have the opportunity to help our children make good choices when we talk to them about small crises like this. By listening to their feelings and suggesting possible solutions, or, better yet, leading them toward coming up with their own solutions, we are steering them away from self-pity and toward self-determination. Our confidence in our children's inner strength will help give them the faith they need to trust in and rely upon themselves. That's more important than an extra measure of "sympathy" any day!

If children live with ridicule, they learn to feel shy

The truth about ridicule is that it's cruel. The falsehood is that it's all in fun. "Oh, come on, I was only kidding. Can't you take a joke?" Rationalizing ridicule in this way effectively blames the victim for any reaction she might show. The person being ridiculed is placed in a no-win position. If she objects to the ridicule, she may be ridiculed even more. If she accepts the ridicule, her self-esteem suffers.

A child who is ridiculed often doesn't know whether it is best to try to appease or to avoid the person picking on her. This confusion results in an ambivalence, a stalemate, like putting the brakes on and stepping on the accelerator of the car simultaneously. Caught in this conflict, the child may become hesitant and shy, hanging out on the fringes of experience, trying not to call attention to herself.

The type of shyness resulting from ridicule is different from a natural inborn quietness that some children show. They seem to need longer to connect to people in new situations and we need to accept that this is part of their personality. But children who become shy and hold back as an attempt to avoid being ridiculed need our help. It's our job to listen, to find out what's going on, and help them figure out ways to deal with the situation.

Cheers or Jeers?

Ridicule and laughter often go together, but they're not natural companions. In fact, ridicule can be seen as a subversion of laughter. At its healthiest and purest, shared laughter can send feelings of well-being and relaxation through our bodies and help bind friendships. On the other hand, ridicule involves making fun of someone. The laughter is at someone's expense. Distinguishing between healthy laughter and the jeers of ridicule is confusing for kids, especially since we laugh at the discomforts of others in cartoons, comics, and movies. If a clown walks into a wall, we giggle. We need to explain to our children that comedy is different than real life, and that in real life we don't laugh when another is hurt or fails, but try to help him. Otherwise kids may not understand that it's wrong to laugh at the troubles of others, and when the crowd hoots at someone's difficulty, they'll hoot, too.

Ten-year-old Scott, who is not an athlete, is taking his turn at bat in the neighborhood baseball game. The kids on the other team begin to chant his name as if cheering him on. "Scott, Scott, Scott," they say. The rhythm builds in intensity.

At first Scott is pleased with the attention. But as he swings and misses once, then twice, he realizes the kids are making fun of him. He becomes confused, then angry. He swings again, and strikes out. The taunting follows him as his team moves into the outfield. By now Scott is red-faced and humiliated. He doesn't know whether to quit the game or ignore the kids and keep playing.

Ridicule contaminates laughter with contempt. This can be confusing to children, young or old. Scott didn't immediately recognize that he was being ridiculed. His natural inclination was to want to participate in the fun the others were having. When he did realize they were making fun of him, embarrassment set in. The insult was initially too subtle for Scott to understand, so he felt bewildered and didn't know how to respond.

If this kind of taunting were directed at him frequently, Scott could easily become discouraged and begin to withdraw from the neighborhood games. Even the fear of being ridiculed is enough to keep some kids on the sidelines, and can lead eventually to a pervasive sense of reticence or shyness. And when a child becomes overly hesitant, a destructive cycle can be set in motion. The other kids sense the child's vulnerability and may pick on him even more, making him the butt of their jokes. This is a painful role for a child to be cast in and a high price to pay for being included in the group. Yet it sometimes may seem that the only alternative is isolation and loneliness.

Our children may not always be able to tell us about experiences such as these. They may feel too humiliated or embarrassed to admit that they have been the object of ridicule. Or they may feel we can't help them. And it's true, we can't protect our children from the taunting of other children since parental intervention would most likely make things even worse. But we can support our children by encouraging them to find the strength to overcome the ridicule and to seek out other friends.

Sometimes we have to recognize that our children are ridiculing others. It's not always easy to be honest with ourselves and face the fact that our children, too, can be cruel. A simple admonishment—"Don't say that," or "That's not polite"—does not adequately address the situation. The child might only be more careful to make sure that we couldn't hear his unkind comments the next time. We can increase his sensitivity to others' feelings by saying, "Imagine how you would feel if so and so said that to you," or "Did you see the look on his face when you said that to him? I wonder how he felt." We need to teach our children empathy and kindness. The best way to do this is to be there for them, to let them know, "I'm with you; I understand." If they've experienced empathy in their own lives, it's much easier for them to be attuned to the needs of others and to treat people gently.

Parental Support

Even though you can't control how other kids treat your children, you can help in other ways. You can be sensitive to any signs that your child may be the object of ridicule by noticing if he becomes suddenly withdrawn, unusually shy, or insecure. If he tells you that other kids are calling him names, insulting or threatening him, take it seriously. Saying things like, "It doesn't matter," "Forget it," "They didn't mean it" doesn't help. Your first move should be to listen and encourage your child to discuss his hurt or confusion. If your child is in preschool or early elementary school, you may want to speak to the teacher, eliciting another source of help. The purpose of such a conversation is not to blame other children, nor to seek protection for your child. Rather, it's to plan a team approach to help him.

Nine-year-old Clare was being consistently rejected and taunted by a group of girls in her fourth-grade classroom. Her teacher noticed she was becoming shy and withdrawn, making her even more vulnerable to ridicule. Clare's mother called the teacher because Clare was crying every night at bedtime and didn't want to go to school in the morning. Her parents and teacher met to discuss how Clare might handle the situation better.

Together they developed a coordinated plan. When Clare and the girls who were taunting her got close to each other, the teacher would gently and as unobtrusively as possible guide Clare away from them and toward a more receptive group of kids. At home, Clare's parents talked with her about the way real friends should treat each other, and discussed ways she could develop new friendships. With help from her parents and teacher, Clare learned how to seek out friends who were truly supportive, and how to best handle situations in which other children were being unkind.

When We're the Culprits

Sometimes, often without thinking, we're the ones who are doing the ridiculing. We may make a sniping comment about a passerby or acquaintance or make a mean-spirited joke at the expense of a friend. We may not feel as if we are really doing anything wrong because we're talking about a stranger or someone who's not present, but if our kids are listening, they'll think it's okay to bad-mouth others.

A mother I know told me the following story. "In our neighborhood shopping center, there is a young woman who sometimes stands at the corner and waves at the passing cars. She's always smiling or singing when she walks by. One day, coming out of the market, there she was. The woman ahead of me said to her daughter, who was about seven, 'There goes the crazy lady.'

"'Mom, that's not nice to say,' The little girl said, clearly upset. 'How would you like it if someone called you crazy?'

"I piped up and said as I was passing, 'I call her the happy lady.' The daughter looked relieved.

"The mom smiled weakly and said, 'I guess she does look happy.'"

Sometimes the child brings the lesson to us.

Ridicule in the Family

As parents, we sometimes fall into the trap of ridiculing or teasing our children, thinking it will toughen them up. Needless to say, ridicule is not a good method for developing strength of character. At best, the child will only end up with a false bravado, trying to protect himself. This is in no way to be mistaken for true inner strength.

Twelve-year-old Pete's father had been a star soccer player in his day, and now Pete was on a local team headed for a championship season. Dad didn't think Pete was aggressive enough on the field, so he tried to motivate him. Unfortunately for Pete, the motivation took the form of ridicule delivered during practice in front of his teammates.

"What're you doing out there? Waiting for tea to be served? Get in there, go after the ball," Dad would yell from the sidelines. Pete would nod and head back out onto the field seething, jaw clenched, too angry and frustrated to concentrate on the game.

Pete's father may have meant well. He may not have

realized his remarks were humiliating and cruel. He may have just been repeating the kinds of things that were said to him when he was playing soccer. Unfortunately, not only did he not help Pete's game, he hurt his relationship with his son.

A more malicious pattern of ridicule is often found between siblings, who can be experts at needling each other through sarcasm, name-calling, and other cruel tactics. Brothers and sisters know each other's vulnerabilities and are experts at aiming them.

Jill knew her younger brother was interested in becoming friends with the new boy in the neighborhood. They both had skateboards and were about the same age. So whenever she saw them hanging out together, she would ride by on her bike, yelling something like, "Hi, Bedwetter. Did you pee in your bed last night?"

This is not just harmless teasing, it is cruel and devastating ridicule. Daily exposure to ridicule within the family is damaging and will leave a child hesitant and shy about participating in his own life. Parents need to be aware of what's really going on between siblings, especially when the parents are not around. They need to step in and set clear limits and consistent consequences, so that all the children in the family will be able to feel safe and comfortable within their own homes.

The Safety of Home

Everyone is the butt of another's jokes or taunts some time, and there's no way we can spare our kids from experiencing at least some level of ridicule at some point in their childhood. But if we make our home a safe haven, our children can rely on it to be a place where they can just be themselves, with minimum pressure. In addition, I believe that parents who accept that they themselves have faults and make mistakes and actively try to learn from them, create a warmer, more lighthearted environment for their children's growth. Their kids learn by example that the world doesn't come to an end when they make a wrong move. Grown-ups are still learning too, and can even laugh at themselves. When family members are able to laugh together, *with*—rather than *at*—each other, shyness can melt away.

If children live with jealousy, they learn to feel envy

Jealousy, the green-eyed monster. The image, with its focus on eyes, reveals the truth about the feeling. Jealousy grows out of how we look at things. We can see our neighbors' grass as greener, their car as better, their house as more impressive. Or we can appreciate and enjoy our own grass, our own car, and our own house.

The reality is, there will always be those who have more of the things we want, but there will always be those who have less, too. It's up to us to decide how to live with that fact. If we are dissatisfied, constantly comparing ourselves with those who have more, and envious of what they have, our children will likely follow in our footsteps, leading lives that are tainted by jealousy and disappointment. We need to tame our own green-eyed monsters, so that our children can learn how to enjoy what they have, rather than be unhappy about what they don't.

Yours Is Better Than Mine

Noticing differences and making comparisons is normal, inevitable, and, in fact, essential to our existence. The ability to discern differences is an important element in the crucial skill of observation. For children, learning to see differences is the first step toward the ability to think critically. It's the conclusions we come to as a result of our comparisons that can lead us into trouble— into the destructive feelings of jealousy and envy.

The kids were playing in the yard and Mom was gardening when Dad pulled into the driveway in a brand-new car. Mom was pleased he had gotten the color she wanted, and the girls were thrilled. It was their first new car, a total surprise. Dad was very proud.

Taking care of the new car was a family effort everyone enjoyed. Over the summer months, the girls helped wash the car on weekends, and when they were riding in it, they were on their good behavior, keeping their shoes off the upholstery and not eating.

That fall, a neighbor bought a new car, a fancier model, at a lower price. When Dad heard the news, he took it hard. "Maybe I should have gone for that model," he said. "If only I'd waited a few months, I would've gotten a better deal."

Mom was reassuring. "It doesn't matter," she said. "Our car is perfect for us."

Dad felt she didn't understand and was not comforted. The children didn't know exactly what the problem was with their wonderful new car all of a sudden, but they definitely recognized a shift in their father's attitude toward it. They saw him looking at the neighbor's car with envy whenever he saw it backing out of the driveway. They knew he was jealous even though they didn't understand why. Sadly, his loss of enthusiasm was contagious. The car no longer felt special to the girls. They began eating snacks in the backseat, brushing crumbs onto the floor. After a while, it didn't look so special anymore, either.

Dad's attitude affected not only his own sense of well-being, but his family's. His jealousy conveyed a message to his daughters that a sense of personal worth is dependent upon ownership and possessions. This is not the kind of message we want to give our children.

Making comparisons doesn't always lead to trouble— it can just as easily lead to appreciation and admiration. If Dad had been able to keep his neighbor's good fortune separate in his mind from his own, he might have been able to respect the neighbor for his bargaining ability and admire his car, while continuing to enjoy his own.

Sometimes it's not material possessions that spark our envy, but other people's kids. This is most likely to happen if we regard our children as extensions of ourselves, and believe that their achievements reflect upon us. Entangling our identities with those of our children sets the stage for making comparisons that lead directly to unhealthy competition. Suddenly, it matters very much to us whose kid walks first, whose makes the team, wins the award, looks the best, has the most friends, and goes to the Ivy League college.

One young mother told me, "I remember listening to another child reading a sophisticated story when my daughter was not yet interested in *The Cat in the Hat*. I was consumed with feelings of jealousy. I found myself not only wishing my child could read like this other child, but that this small, innocent four-year-old would hit a three-syllable word and fall silent. At this point, I realized the viciousness in my envy, and I didn't like what I saw."

There will always be children who are better, faster, smarter, or more attractive than our children, giving us unlimited opportunities to be envious. But here again, we can choose how to look at the situation. Instead of seeing our children's inabilities, it's far better to focus on their strengths. Then when comparisons inevitably arise, we will be able to appreciate what is special about each child. In addition, we must recognize that our children's successes and failures are their own, not ours. We love our kids, and it's only natural that we rejoice when they succeed and feel pain when they don't. But we must make sure that our hopes and expectations for our kids are tailored to *their* personalities and strengths, not to our own unfulfilled wishes for ourselves.

Sibling Rivalry

It's natural for siblings to compete for parental attention or praise. Comparing siblings or, worse yet, favoring one child over another, makes this normal competition far more intense, and reduces the chances for siblings to be friends later in life.

Mom was trying to encourage seven-year-old Sharon. "I hope you'll work harder on your handwriting," she said. "If you practice, you could have beautiful penmanship like your sister."

Sharon looked across the dining room table at her ten-year-old sister, who was quietly doing her homework. The teachers liked her more, the kids liked her more, even Mom liked her more. Sharon didn't know whether to hate her sister or herself.

"I can't do anything right. My pencil smudges. And I hate learning to write," she burst out, and ran upstairs to her room to cry.

When a child reacts this negatively to something we've said, it's a signal to us to examine our intentions. Mom's first impulse here was to feel defensive, to wonder why her daughter was being so unreasonable. But if she took time to consider, she'd realize she'd made an unfair comparison and had sparked Sharon's jealousy of her sister. Mom needs to understand her daughter's feelings and to apologize to her. Children are surprisingly generous in their capacity to forgive, especially when parents are willing to admit their mistakes. Just as importantly, she needs to let Sharon know that from now on she won't compare Sharon to anyone but herself.

The reality is, even if we're on the ball every second (and no one can be), monitoring our every utterance, we still won't be able to avoid sibling rivalry. Most common sibling jealousies are very basic. Mom is slicing cake for dessert. Linda and Gary, five-year-old twins, are watching her like hawks, both ready to protest if they feel short-changed. Now, it's very difficult to make cake slices perfectly even. Someone always seems to end up with a bigger piece or more icing. But it's important to try your best. We may smile at the smallness of this example, but these moments are exactly the kind that accumulate over a childhood, leaving some children feeling, "Mom always loved you more."

Take your children's feelings of jealousy seriously, and whenever possible, do what you can to balance the situation. Remember, the cake is a symbol of parental love and attention. By emphasizing their need for equal pieces of cake, the children may be indirectly expressing their need to feel loved in equal amounts. Rather than make them feel silly, we can respond to those needs generously, paving the way for them to do the same for others.

The Pack Mentality

"Suzanne streaks her hair. Why can't I?"

"But Mickey got a pair of those sneakers . . ."

"Everybody has pierced ears. I want mine pierced, too."

Kids of all ages can be envious of others, wishing they had what the others have—clothes, friends, grades, a car, curly hair, straight hair. They think that if they have the same things, they'll become like the friends they admire. "With the right clothes, I'll be popular like Samantha" or "When I get new high-tops, I'll play basketball as well as Jason does."

It's easy for children to confuse skills and possessions with well-being. They think they need to have certain things to become popular or athletic, and believe this is the way to feel good about themselves. Unfortunately, this approach to life only sets the stage for disappointment, as most of us have learned the hard way.

During the preteen and teenage years, when kids are more focused on their peers than their parents, they may become obsessed with having the right possessions. This is also the time when kids are learning to think abstractly and philosophically, and are beginning to define their place in the world. This process can be a little daunting, to say the least: teens may take refuge from the confusion in "the group." Fitting in can become paramount.

We need to help kids recognize that individual

differences are okay, and in fact are to be desired. We want our kids to develop enough confidence in themselves that they don't feel the need to resort to copying other kids or hankering for certain possessions in an effort to belong. A teenager with a strong self-image will have less of a need to emulate others.

This doesn't mean that kids shouldn't be influenced by their friends. Modeling oneself after an admired friend is different from mimicking him, and admiration can lead our children into setting goals for themselves and achieving things they might not otherwise have done. Even when she doesn't meet her goal, a teenager whose inspiration is appreciation and admiration, not envy, will be better able to see the bigger picture. "Carmen got captain. I'm disappointed, but she'll do a great job. It looks like our team's going to be really strong this year. We're looking to be undefeated," says Carrie, who'd been hoping to be elected captain of her high-school track team.

Teenagers need our help as they explore who they are. As they make their way through the minefield of adolescence, it is very important for us to be available to them. We can help them identify their best qualities and learn how to express them. The best way to do this is by listening, often at odd moments—riding in the car, before they go to sleep, while making cookies or doing yard work together. These are the moments that can't be planned and it's part of the reason that "quality time" can't always be scheduled in advance. The key is to listen to them as they express their thoughts and feelings, and to offer them our own perspective in a way that is sensitive to their increasing need for independence. When our children open up to us, we need to be careful to hear them out, then share our perspective, rather than simply telling them what to do. We want to encourage independent thinking in our teenagers, not compliance.

Valuing Our Children, Valuing Ourselves

As parents, we have a choice in how we see our children, and we have the responsibility to choose to see and appreciate what is unique in each child. When we value our children, they learn to value themselves. By paying attention and listening closely to their wishes, worries, dreams, jokes, and desires, we let them know they are important to us, that we love them and appreciate their own unique qualities, and that we wouldn't want them to be any other kind of person.

We can also help them to accept themselves for who they are by showing them that we accept ourselves—with all our own unique qualities, and our weaknesses as well as our strengths. There is no better reason to finally make peace with ourselves and come to terms with our own imperfections than this: that by our own examples we can help our children learn to accept themselves and make their lives the very best they can.

If children live with shame, they learn to feel guilty

We want our children to know right from wrong. Learning this will take them all the years they are with us, if not a lifetime. We may begin by teaching our kids that they should not take toys from friends, that we must pay for the gum at the store, and that cheating is unfair and wrong. As they get older, we may help them wrestle with more complicated ethical questions—whether it's ever okay to lie, what to do if they know a friend has done something wrong, and so on. Developing a strong internal moral compass is a life-long process, but we can help our kids get a good start.

How do we help our children learn to distinguish right from wrong? We hope they will learn to be good and kind by following our example, but how should we respond when they aren't? What do we do when their behavior is decidedly wrong? What do we do if they harm another person or intentionally destroy property? We want them to understand that we won't knowingly allow them to harm another or themselves. We also want them to see where they went wrong, to feel ashamed of themselves, to regret their actions, and even to suffer the consequences, so they'll learn from their mistakes.

Yet we don't want our children to live with shame and guilt. Blaming and shaming kids makes them feel bad about themselves, and can lead to a lack of self-confidence or a general feeling of unworthiness. So we should not overuse shame to manipulate or control our children. Children learn best from support and encouragement, not punishment.

Fortunately, most of us are not dealing with kids who deliberately try to hurt others or damage things. Usually it's our kids' unintentional, unthinking transgressions that call for our intervention—the times when they grab a toy out of a friend's hands, leave the kitchen a mess, or borrow things without asking. When these things occur, it's our job as parents to help them understand how they came to choose a wrong action and to point out how they can take responsibility for their behavior and set things right.

Encouraging Learning, Not Guilt

When our children do something wrong—when they steal, lie, cheat—our first impulse may be anger, and then, unfortunately, to assume the worst. At these moments it's important to give our children the benefit of the doubt. They may not fully understand the ethical rules they are breaking. Instead of berating or scolding them, we can turn these incidences into learning experiences. If we are careful not to jump to conclusions, but instead let our children tell us why they did what they did, we can ensure that they come away from the experience with a better idea of what is expected of them, and with their sense of self worth intact.

Mom notices that her wallet is open inside her pocketbook, and that all her spare change is gone. She and her seven-year-old daughter, Melissa, are alone in the house. Mom goes to Melissa's room and, taking care to stick to the facts, says "I noticed that all the coins are gone from my wallet."

Melissa, busy with her dolls, looks up.

Mom continues, "My wallet was left open inside my purse. Usually I close it. I wonder how that happened."

Melissa tries to explain. "Well the ice-cream truck came and I needed some money to buy a popsicle, and you were busy on the phone, so I just helped myself. I couldn't close the zipper on the wallet, though. Sorry."

Mom is tempted to smile, but she maintains a serious face. It's nice that Melissa is sorry, but she's sorry for the wrong thing. Mom sits down next to Melissa and her dolls and says gently but firmly, "My pocketbook and my money are private. I don't take money from you and you're not allowed to take it from me."

If this is the first incident of its kind, Mom and Melissa may agree that Melissa can pay back her mom from her allowance. If it's the second time, the consequence may also include giving up a favorite TV show. (If taking money is a pattern, then Mom needs to determine a more serious course of action, maybe even seek professional help to find out what's at the root of Melissa's stealing.)

Mom does not shame Melissa for taking the money, but she does make it clear that her behavior is wrong and is unacceptable. Melissa may feel guilty for her behavior, but she doesn't have to feel that she is a bad person.

Mom could help Melissa learn how to handle the situation better next time by saying, "I understand you wanted the money for ice cream and I was busy. But you can't take money from my wallet without asking. What could you have done instead?"

Melissa thinks hard, then says "I could've waited, but the ice-cream truck would have left." She pauses, then adds, "I guess I could have gotten the money from my piggy bank."

"Yes, you could have," Mom agrees.

"I could have written you a note for you to read while you were on the phone."

"That's another possibility."

"I could have not gotten the ice cream," Melissa offers hesitantly, and not very enthusiastically.

"I don't think so," Mom laughs and gives Melissa a hug. "But next time ask me first if you want money, okay?"

Mom's questions lead Melissa through a valuable lesson in evaluating her behavior and thinking of how she could have satisfied her desire for the ice cream in a way that was acceptable. These questions do not make her feel bad about herself by instilling shame or guilt. Instead, they may help her feel better about herself as she takes more responsibility for her actions.

Shame on You

The mess in Julie's bedroom is totally out of control. Her mom has reached her limit of tolerance. In a voice designed to make the eleven-year-old feel bad about herself, she says, "What's wrong with you? How can you live in this pigsty? You're a disgrace."

Julie falls into a dejected slump, heads for her room, and says, "Oh, all right!" Then she cleans up her room.

However, even after Julie has done what her mother wanted her to do, she still feels that there's something wrong with her. Using shame to control a child's behavior only teaches the child to feel bad about herself. It takes the fun out of pleasing Mom, and it doesn't necessarily lead to the desired long-term changes in behavior.

Julie's mom needs to remember that the room was a mess, not her daughter. A clear, "I want you to clean up your room right now" communicates her disapproval while allowing Julie to preserve her sense of self-worth.

Even adding, "It's a disaster area, and I can't stand it any longer" makes it clear that it is the mess that is upsetting, not the child.

Children's Rights to Their Feelings

As adults, we may have a hard time remembering what it is like to be a child. Sometimes when our kids get upset or angry, it seems to us that they're being silly or irrational. We have to remember that children are learning to express their feelings and aren't yet able to rationalize or compartmentalize them. We need to let them express themselves without being shamed, whether their feelings seem sensible to us or not.

Donny was an active, bright five-year-old who was extremely frightened by thunder and lightning. Unfortunately, where he lived there were frequent and dramatic thunderstorms. Each time a storm would build, Donny's fear would escalate. He'd start by saying "I'm afraid. The thunder sounds so close. Can the lightning hit us here?" Then he'd progress through whimpering, crying, all-out screaming, and finally, ducking for cover.

Donny's father couldn't stand the fact that his son was afraid, needing to be comforted and protected. At first he would try to calm Donny. "There's nothing to be afraid of," he would say. "Don't worry, the lightning can't get you in here."

When this didn't help, Donny's father would repeat the

same message louder, with growing impatience. This made things even worse: Donny would become more frightened, and his father more irritated. Finally at the end of his rope, Dad would burst out, "I'd be ashamed of myself if I were you! What's wrong with you anyway?" Now Donny's father wasn't just minimizing Donny's fears; he was teaching his son to be ashamed of feeling afraid.

Donny's dad would have had better luck if he'd been able to accept Donny's fears. He could have taken his son into his lap and said something like, "Hey, what would you like to say to Mr. Thunder and Mr. Lightning?" This would encourage Donny to address his fears constructively, rather than just dramatizing them. Donny might even have discovered he could conquer his fear by yelling right back at the thunder, "Go away!"

Our kind acceptance of our children's faults and fears, and our help as they face them, allows them to grow up feeling good about themselves, rather than ashamed. No matter how off-base some of these feelings may seem to us, each child has a basic right to express his feelings and to have his emotional needs met. As the child grows, this right is balanced by his responsibility to express himself in ways that are appropriate and respectful of others. But until he has gained this maturity, there is nothing to be gained in trying to shame him into pretending that the feelings are not there. Allowing him to express his real feelings is the first step toward his resolution of them.

When our children are allowed to tell us the way they really feel, we are able to help them to discharge negative feelings, move forward, and grow.

Accepting Responsibility

Young children learn a lot about cause and effect through experimentation and play. A toddler who drops her spoon from her high chair is experimenting. For her, it's fun—even more so when Mom or Dad retrieves the spoon each time, so she can drop it again. She enjoys her role in the cause and effect game, and only gives it up when the other player breaks the cycle by refusing to pick up the spoon.

As children mature, they gain understanding of more subtle ways they can cause an event, as well as how it may affect others. This learning is the beginning of the responsibility and accountability that naturally evolve along with children's increased participation in family life. Children don't need to feel shame in order to be concerned about how things will turn out or to want to make amends. Even young children often express a spontaneous desire to help make things right again. Fortunately, most children want to please their parents most of the time.

Six-year-old Billy was getting the orange juice out of the refrigerator when the carton slipped through his little hands and fell to the floor. From his eighteen-month-old sister's point of view in the high chair, it made a wonderful crash and splash. She clapped her hands in excitement. Billy saw the situation with a more mature eye and realized what a mess he had made and the trouble he was in. He grabbed a kitchen towel and began sloshing it through the puddle of orange juice. His intention was to soak up the juice, but he didn't realize he would have to wring out the towel to do this effectively. To his mother, it looked like Billy was just playing with the juice on the floor.

Billy looked up at her, his hands and knees sticky with orange juice. "I'm sorry, Mommy," he said. "I'm cleaning it up."

His mother took a deep breath before saying anything, and saw that Billy was doing his best to mop up the puddle. "Let me help you," she said. "You're off to a good start, but we'll do better with a sponge and a bucket."

It's vitally important to notice and praise the efforts our children make to help restore a situation. We want to recognize and encourage their budding ability to take responsibility, rather than punish them for their shortcomings. Billy recognized his mistake, apologized, and tried his best to fix things up. He may not have been entirely effective, but his efforts were in the right direction. His mother accepted his apology and his efforts at improving things. Because she did, Billy and his mother were able to move gracefully through what might have been an unpleasant situation, and to experience a positive cycle of apology, the taking of responsibility, and forgiveness. Together, they cleaned up the kitchen and they bolstered good feelings about each other in the process.

We also need to let our kids know that responsibility is a two-sided coin. We want them to accept responsibility when they have made a mistake, but also to accept it when they have done something well. This will allow them to draw strength and pride from their accomplishments, and will help them to keep working on the things that need improving.

Sorry About That

Apologies can act as a balm, helping heal a situation in which someone or something has been hurt. When, during a rousing game of dodgeball, twelve-year-old Andrew threw the ball so hard that it knocked a classmate over, he ran to her side.

"Are you okay?" he asked. "I'm really sorry. I didn't mean to hurt you. Do you want me to help you to the nurse's office?" He accepted responsibility for what had happened, was genuinely sorry for causing the girl pain, and was willing to help her out.

Some children, on the other hand, use apology like a magic wand, as if by apologizing they can erase their role in causing a problem. They seem to feel no guilt or shame. They act as if the apology gives them a green light to continue their actions uninterrupted, or that it's an easy route to attaining forgiveness, assuming that the response to any apology will be, "Oh, that's all right. I understand." One nine-year-old boy had devised a rather cynical method of apologizing. He wrote out signed chits saying, "I'm sorry" ahead of time. Then whenever he got into trouble in the classroom or on the playground, he simply handed over one of these generic apologies to the offended party. When an apology is offered carelessly, or even flippantly, we need to let our children know that it will not suffice.

We want our children to recognize that their actions affect others, and that when they do something that hurts or offends someone—whether intentionally or not—it's important to understand how the person may be feeling and to recognize their role in causing pain. This will lead to heartfelt apologies and an attempt to set things right, as opposed to a casually tossed-off "Sorry." A sincere apology includes the acceptance of responsibility and a genuine feeling of regret, as well as the intention to make things better in the future.

We can help kids develop the important attribute of empathy by listening to them carefully ourselves. When children feel that we are trying to understand how they feel, it's easier for them to try to understand how others may be feeling. Four-year-old Sam rode his tricycle into his older brother Casey's elaborate tower of blocks. After removing Sam from the scene and giving him a "time-out" his father sat down with him and asked him what had made him destroy Casey's tower.

Sam said he was frustrated that Casey wasn't playing with him.

"How do you think Casey feels about his tower being ruined?" Dad asked.

"Sad and mad," Sam said.

Dad then asked Sam whether he thought smashing Casey's tower was a good way to get his brother to play with him. Sam admitted it wasn't, and he and Dad talked about better ways for Sam to get Casey's attention. Dad also asked Sam how he could try to fix the situation. Sam said he would tell Casey he was sorry and help him rebuild the tower.

Sam apologized to Casey, and Casey grudgingly accepted his apology. Although Casey not surprisingly refused Sam's offer to help rebuild the tower, he realized his little brother was trying to make amends and in his own way appreciated it.

Respect for Others—and Themselves

Our children need our assurance and guidance to take their place in a world of rules and regulations. In giving these, we must remember that shame and guilt are strong feelings and should be used sparingly. Likewise, we should bear in mind that placing blame doesn't necessarily promote desired behavior in children, whereas seeing their role in causing an effect and being held accountable for their actions often does.

Given an abundance of positive, respectful reinforcement, most children come to understand that they are responsible for the consequences of their actions. They become more responsible as they understand the nature of cause and effect. They see the connection between what they did and what happened, and they want to help set things right.

The ability to see ahead and evaluate possible outcomes takes time to develop (waiting while it does may require patience for all in the family). As our children mature, they come to respect their inner sense of right and wrong, and to understand that sometimes when something goes amiss, it is due to their wrong action. They are more able to respect the feelings of others and to sincerely apologize for their mistake or offense, and can receive forgiveness for it. This completes a cycle that emphasizes learning from within, rather than learning through shame or guilt.

If children live with encouragement, they learn confidence

The root meaning of the word encouragement is "to give heart." When we encourage our children, we give them courage from our hearts to theirs. It is our job to help and support them while they develop the skills and confidence they need to stand on their own. This can be a very delicate matter: Knowing when to step in and when to step aside, when to praise and when to offer constructive criticism is an art, not a science.

Our children need our support, but they also need our honest assessment of their progress as they work at developing and refining their many skills. They need us to help move them forward as well as be there for them when they've fallen back. They need us to encourage them to expand their limits and broaden their horizons, to urge them to do better than they thought they could. At the same time they need to know that we're on their side, even when they fail.

In order to do all this, we need to pay careful attention to each child's unique needs, talents, and desires. Recognizing children's individual differences—how this one deals with discouragement or distractions, how well that one is able to sustain interest in a project, which child needs more help and guidance, and which one works better independently—is key to giving each of them effective, concrete guidance as they strive to reach their goals.

The Many Ways to Encourage

It's natural to offer praise for a job well done, but it's also important to recognize and praise our children for the little steps they take toward their goals. It may be too much to ask three-year-old Samantha to be nice to her baby brother all the time. But when the mood strikes her and she pats his hand tenderly, or turns her attention to making him laugh during a ride in the car, it's important to acknowledge her thoughtfulness. "Look how happy you've made him!" Mom notices, and Samantha feels happy, too—and proud!

We can also encourage our children by helping them reach their goals, and there are many ways to do this. Sometimes it's better to reach out to help them before a situation overwhelms them, and sometimes it's better to stand back and let them solve their own problems. But even when we are leaving them to their own devices, we can be there with a few kind words, a pat on the back, or a well-timed suggestion.

When our children are frustrated, we can focus on the

aspect of the project that they have accomplished, or the difficulty of what they've attempted, rather than the fact that they haven't succeeded yet in what they set out to do.

Nathan, who is five, is building a tower of blocks. He's created an elaborate structure but it's also a delicate one, and it's bound to fall down soon. When it does, he bursts into tears and wails of frustration. Fortunately, Dad is ready with an encouraging word. "I noticed that you built a really tall building that time. Almost as tall as you," he says. "Would you like some help getting another one started?" As they work together on the new tower, Dad shows Nathan some techniques he can use to make the structure sturdier. Nathan has the satisfaction of knowing that his previous attempt was noticed and appreciated, and now he's learning new skills that will help him make better block towers in the future.

Encouraging our kids involves more than simply praising them. Fourteen-year-old Suzy is working on a history report on the Salem witch trials. Her father is glad to see how engaged she is in the project, and that she has taken the time to pull together a lot of different source material. However, all her research has left her floundering amidst too much information, and the report is due in two days.

"Wow, looks like you've done a lot of work and gathered a lot information," Dad says to Suzy.

Suzy replies, "I have. I'll never get through it all."

"Which of these materials seem like the ones that

you'll use the most?" Dad asks. "Why don't you concentrate on those first, and if you have time, go back and use the others?"

Suzy looks up with interest, and Dad can practically see her mind working. "These three books are best," she says, with excitement and some relief, "I'll put the other stuff aside for now."

Dad helped Suzy in exactly the way she needed. Because he noticed that the project was in trouble and took the time to help Suzy think through a solution, he was able to help her recover and complete the report on time. This kind of help is far more meaningful than reflexively saying, "Nice job."

Traps We Fall Into

Encouraging our kids is not always easy. When they are small, it takes more time to let them do things for themselves than it would take for us to do it for them. When they're older, it may not be a question of time, but of effort—we may tire of struggling to get our children to do things they should do for themselves. But no matter how old they are, we should not fall into the trap of doing things for them. It's important for our children to learn to be responsible and to participate in the tasks of daily life in accordance with their age and abilities. And it is our job to encourage them to do it.

Barry is learning how to tie his shoes. His stubby four-year-old fingers are having trouble looping the laces through. Mom is watching him with growing impatience. They're running late, and she's thinking she should have bought the Velcro sneakers.

"Here, let me help," she says. She pushes his hands aside, and quickly ties the shoe herself. Her hands move so fast, Barry can't see how she did it. He wants to do it himself, so he pulls at the strings, and undoes her work so he can start over. Now it's even later, they're both frustrated and angry with each other, and they still haven't gotten anywhere with the shoes.

As parents, it's important for us to try to arrange our schedules in such a way that our children have the time they need to work at mastering the things they are learning—how to dress themselves, brush their teeth, tidy their room—with a minimum of pressure and hurrying. With the stressful lives many of us lead, getting everyone up a half-hour, or even an hour earlier, may seem too high a price to pay. Certainly for many parents, juggling the multiple demands of home and work, it may not always be possible. That is of course for every parent to decide. But in weighing the decision, think about how important this matter is for your child—she needs to learn to do things for herself, and she needs to be able to do so in such a way that she can feel proud and confident of her accomplishments, not ashamed and frustrated by her inability to keep up with the frantic pace of things.

Another trap we may fall into is in trying to protect our kids from failure, disappointment, or harm, unintentionally discouraging them from trying new things. We don't want our children to be hurt, yet there are times we need to allow them to take a risk.

Eddie has decided to run for president of his sixth-grade class. One night, after Eddie is asleep, his mom and dad discuss the upcoming election.

"He'll be crushed if he doesn't win," Mom worries. "I never should have encouraged him to start this whole thing."

Dad laughs, "He'll be fine. It's a good experience for him."

"Even if he loses?" Mom asks.

"Especially if he loses," Dad responds.

Dad's right. Eddie will learn and grow stronger from his experience, whatever the election results. If he wins he will obviously gain self-confidence. If he loses, he will at least have the satisfaction that goes with knowing he has given his best effort to realize a goal that is important to him. Mom needs to shift her role from protecting her son to encouraging his growth, even when the outcome may be painful for both of them.

Another pitfall of parenting may lie in the phrase "just try it." When we encourage our children to "just try" something new—a dreaded vegetable, an unpleasant task—we may be unwittingly giving them the message that they can get by with a quick attempt and nothing more. For the child who is looking for an easy out, having "just tried" can be an excuse to stop before finishing what needs to be done.

When our children are faced with a challenging situation, it's better to focus on their potential, rather than the least we expect of them. When you encourage your child to "Do the best you can," you let him know what you would like him to do, without pressuring him. By asking your child to do his best, you are expressing faith in his ability, and paving the way for him to succeed. Creating a climate of positive expectations is important. It's also a fairly safe bet, since with practice, learning, and greater maturity, most kids will make progress at just about anything.

Finally, we need to be careful not to push our children to fulfill our own unmet goals. Mom has persuaded the school to place her daughter in an honors math class. Tiffany is struggling, but Mom's determined. "You need this class to get into an Ivy League college," she says. "You can do it if you work hard enough."

Tiffany is miserable and doesn't care about getting into an Ivy League college. If Mom were to take the time to let Tiffany talk about the trouble she's having, and to discuss how and why going to an Ivy League college might be to her advantage, she might or might not be able to persuade her that the extra effort was worth it. But by assuming that her daughter's goals are the same as hers, and by minimizing the difficulty Tiffany is having keeping up with the class, Mom is exerting too much pressure. She thinks she's encouraging her daughter, but really she's ignoring Tiffany's needs and trying to live through her.

We need to appreciate and respect our children's own vision of their lives. They do not necessarily see the world as we see it, nor should they. Each child is a unique spirit, with his or her own special gifts to offer. If we encourage them to become the people they want to be, we will have the great privilege of glimpsing the world through their eyes. When we allow them to give the gift of themselves, they grow in confidence, and our world is made richer and fuller.

Our Children's Dreams

When children dream, they dream big. In their dreams, anything is possible. While learning that it almost always takes a tremendous amount of work to make dreams come true is an important part of growing up, we don't want our children to lose the power of their dreams to inspire them in the process. They know no limits and often feel no fear. These qualities are ones we want to help them sustain as we gently guide them toward realistic assessment of the match between their skills and their desires, their abilities and their dreams.

Some of their dreams may seem small to us. "I'm going

to help decorate the Christmas tree this year, and I'm going to put the star on the top," announces three-year-old Sasha. She's becoming a big girl and she wants to participate more fully in an important family ritual. We know she can't reach the top of the tree by herself—but we also know if Dad holds her up, she can do it. "Great idea, Sasha!" says Mom. She focuses on the aspiration, not the fact that Sasha will need help in achieving it. From this experience, Sasha learns that her parents value her dreams, and that they will be there to help her make them come true.

Other dreams are much bigger. We know that not all of our children's dreams are realistic: how do we decide which ones to encourage and which to discourage?

Travis wanted to be a singer, but he had no musical background and couldn't carry a tune. Nevertheless, his father listened to his plans for a musical career seriously, never mentioning his obvious deficits. He encouraged Travis in his dream because he believed in his son and in the importance of doing what you love.

After graduation, Travis moved to Los Angeles, wrote rap lyrics, and connected with a group. In time, they produced a CD. Today, despite his success in entering the world of his dreams, Travis is a "starving artist," not an easy role to maintain. He may decide to move away from music to another career entirely. But even if he does, the important thing is that he had a dream, and his dad encouraged him to "go for it." For the rest of his life, no matter what else he does, he'll know that he gave his dream his best shot. Because he tried, he will be able to live his life without regret, without wishing that he had made the effort, and wondering what might have happened if he had.

Encouraging the Whole Child

Helping our children to become self-reliant is not just about encouraging behavior. We need to think about what inner qualities our children are developing too. When we see our child manifesting a quality we admire— whether it's generosity, kindness, sensitivity, determination, or anything else—we ought to let her know that we notice and appreciate it. Our comments will help shape the self-image our children carry with them into school, the community, and eventually the workplace. When we provide them with a supportive environment, a safe and nurturing place in which to learn, we give them a chance to become the best they can be.

We encourage our children when we support them in what they want to accomplish in their lives. We may introduce suggestions or help guide them along the way, but we should always respect their autonomy, and honor their right to make their own choices. Our role is to be with them through their failures and successes, trusting that they will gain from their experiences and grow in self-confidence no matter what the outcome.

We need to believe in our children's dreams even when we don't completely understand them. We need to believe in our children too, especially when they have lost faith in themselves. Our heartfelt encouragement of our children—their dreams, their strengths, and their inner qualities—will help them develop into adults who can face the world with confidence.

If children live with tolerance, they learn patience

Patience requires tolerance. By tolerance, we mean actively accepting what's happening, not just grudgingly "putting up with it." When we accept the things we cannot change, and decide to make the best of a bad situation instead of gritting our teeth and complaining about it, we may be surprised at the results. A positive attitude not only makes dealing with difficult situations more bearable, it can actually change the ultimate outcome.

A few days before she was to start seventh grade, Keisha broke her leg. While all the other kids were reuniting after the summer vacation, Keisha lay on the sofa at home with her leg in a cast.

Keisha had a choice about how to deal with her circumstances. She had every right to feel miserable, lonely, and impatient. On the other hand, she could choose to accept what had happened and respond to the situation creatively. With her mom's help, Keisha decided to have a cast-signing party. A few of her closest friends came over after school to decorate her cast, eat brownies, drink lemonade, and share gossip. By taking charge of an upsetting situation and deciding not to let it get the best of her, Keisha was able to turn it into a memorable time for herself and her friends.

The Many Moods of Waiting

Waiting patiently is hard to do, even for grown-ups. We develop patience, or at least learn to hide our impatience, because we know that it is socially unacceptable to do otherwise. For small children, waiting is especially difficult. They don't care yet about what others think, so they express their impatience openly. In addition, their limited comprehension of time makes it difficult for them to gauge how long they will have to wait for something. "How much longer?" "Can we go now?" "Are we there yet?" "When is it time?" These are questions that reveal how difficult it is for small children not only to wait, but even to understand the general framework of time passing.

Everyday life provides an abundance of opportunities to teach our children how to wait patiently. "I'm hungry!" a child cries impatiently. As we're preparing his food, we can explain to him that the pasta needs to be cooked, the vegetables need to be cut, the orange must be peeled first. "I want an ice cube!" another child demands. By showing her the ice tray and explaining that it takes time for the water to freeze, we help her understand why she has to wait, and give her a science lesson at the same time. We can listen when our children express their impatience, and let them know we understand how hard it can be to wait, while explaining that some things take time, and that we need to learn to be patient while the necessary steps are being taken.

Waiting in line at the grocery store or going on long car rides are particularly challenging situations for kids. But these times too can provide them with valuable lessons in learning how to wait. We can help by showing them ways to make the time pass agreeably: waiting in line may present an opportunity to chat about school or a recent activity that we haven't yet had a chance to discuss. Car rides can be made much more pleasant when we bring or make up games to play along the way. Even very young children can pass the time more happily when they have something interesting to do: for example, counting all the trucks, red cars, or white houses they see.

It's not only the "nuisance-waiting" that is difficult for children. It's hard for them to wait for the good things in their lives, too. For children, holidays are major events that they look forward to, and they seem to take forever to come! However, their anticipation of the event can be used to help them learn a great deal about the passage of time, and the meaning of a day, a week, a month. We can help them enjoy the waiting period and learn from it, too. Studying the calendar will help them begin to understand how time is represented graphically, and will give them a rudimentary awareness of the relative length of units of time. Preschoolers may enjoy having their very own calendars, and using stickers to mark the special days they are looking forward to. As the time draws nearer, they can be engaged in activities that will help make the event, when it finally comes, more special—creating Christmas and Hanukkah decorations, baking special holiday treats, making gifts for the birthday of a loved one.

Waiting Gracefully

If we ourselves are easily upset by the minor interruptions and inconveniences inherent in everyday living, it will be hard to teach our children how to be patient. As adults, most of us have learned to tolerate trying situations with some degree of composure. Though it's not always easy to do, it is important for us to try to meet these daily challenges gracefully, providing a good example for our children.

On their way home, Dad and ten-year-old Eric find themselves stuck in a traffic jam. The cars are barely moving and, of course, some drivers are switching lanes, edging over to try to get an advantage.

"Why don't you cut in there, Dad? That lane's moving faster," Eric urges his father.

Dad tries to put their situation into perspective for his

son. "It's not really worth changing lanes," he says. "Accidents happen that way. Nobody's going anywhere, so we might as well just relax."

Dad is teaching his son to accept an annoying situation with equanimity. He does more than just stay calm: he also explains the reasoning process that helps him to wait patiently when there's nothing he can do to change the situation. Needless to say, this is much better than complaining, getting frustrated, or yelling at other drivers.

There are some times in our lives when it is harder to be patient— when we are waiting for the birth of a baby, a family member is in surgery, we are anxiously waiting to hear whether we got the new job. These are potentially life-changing events that can upset both parents and children. But these times are also a normal part of life, and the way we respond to them will teach our children how to handle themselves in stressful situations.

Learning how to calm ourselves and be quiet inwardly when we are surrounded by chaos is a gift we can pass on to our children. Even in times of crisis, we can use the time we're waiting to focus ourselves and collect our strength for whatever lies ahead. Taking a brief "quiet time-out" can be practiced almost anywhere: Close your eyes if you can, take a few slow deep breaths—one for vitality, one for energy, one for well-being, and one for calmness. This simple exercise can work wonders in restoring inner strength when we really need it and provides support for active waiting.

When we are in a tense spot, another trick that can help alleviate the situation is to ask ourselves, "What does this situation need? What can I bring to this situation? How can I help make the waiting easier?" Sometimes this enables us to shift our focus away from our worries to a concrete action that will keep us busy and may help the people around us. One woman I know who was waiting to hear from her doctor about the results of a biopsy decided to wash all her windows. "Being active kept my mind off my fears, plus at the end I had sparkling windows that let the sunlight in better and cheered the whole house up," she said.

Sometimes, if we allow them to, our children can even help show us the way. One young mother remembered a time her five-year-old daughter gave her just the kind of support she needed. "I was worried sick about the baby, who was running a high fever," she said. "Molly put her arms around me and said, 'Don't worry, Mommy, Johnny's going to be okay.' She helped me pull myself together, and kept me from panicking. I knew I had to stay strong for both her sake and the baby's."

Learning Patience From Mother Nature

One of the best ways to teach small children about the passing of time is to grow plants. Tending and nurturing a small plant, waiting for each new sprout to appear, gives children a concrete way to begin to understand and make sense of the passage of time. The emergence of a living thing into the world becomes an exciting event and teaches our children that growing takes time and nature cannot be rushed.

Tommy's first-grade class is growing tomato plants at school. Every week, he gives his mom a report on how tall the plants are, and who gets to water them. One day Tommy reports enthusiastically, "We had to give the plants stakes today, so they wouldn't fall over."

His mother is listening politely, somewhat preoccupied with her to-do list. "When do you think you'll get tomatoes?" she asks.

Tommy is taken aback by her question, since he is focused on watching the plants grow. "When they're ready, I guess," he answers.

Almost instantly, Tommy's mother realizes that in her preoccupation, she has skipped over the most important part of the lesson. Tommy is excited about the gradual maturing of the plants, and is noticing small changes along the way. He knows the tomatoes will emerge in due time, but that isn't the goal for him. He is enjoying the life cycle of the plant.

"I think it's wonderful that you're learning all about how plants grow," she says to him. "Isn't it exciting to see them change from day to day?" Tommy looks at his mother and smiles, reassured and happy to see that she does, after all, understand.

Appreciating Our Differences

We often use the word tolerance in the context of discussing racial, religious, or cultural differences. In our families and in our neighborhoods, our tolerance, or intolerance, of human diversity is revealed in the way we treat people who are different from us: both in the way we interact with them directly, and what we say about them when they're not around. Our children notice even the most subtle of innuendos, and while they may not understand the full implication of our words, they pick up our attitudes and mimic our behavior.

Michael's new fifth-grade teacher is of a different race, and Michael's mother seems to have more questions than usual for her son. "What do you think of your new teacher?" she asks. "What books is he recommending? Does he favor some kids over others?"

Michael doesn't understand why his mother's questions are so intense, but he tries to describe the teacher to her as well as he can. "He lets us decorate one bulletin board any way we want to," he says, "and he comes out in the playground with us during recess."

This doesn't seem to satisfy his mother. She persists, "Do you think he's a good teacher? Should we try and move you over to the other classroom?"

Now Michael is really confused. At first he liked the new teacher, but now he's not sure. The next day he walks into class with a slightly different attitude. Maybe this teacher is favoring some kids in the class. He certainly isn't favoring Michael. He'll have to think about this.

If we asked Michael's mother if she was tolerant of other races, she would probably answer, "Yes, of course." Yet she is clearly giving her son a different message.

Our children are growing up in a world where getting along with our global neighbors and sharing the environment, commercial trade, and a planetary fate will be inescapable facts of life. Our kids will need to be comfortable with people of different colors, cultures, abilities, and beliefs. By providing our children with a model of acceptance and tolerance we can teach them to not only respect, but value and even enjoy differences among people, rather than being suspicious of them.

Family Harmony

The family provides our children with their first experience of living and working together in a community. Even within the family, differences abound. What pleases one may upset another. Developing respect for one another and learning to accept, and even appreciate, our differences, takes a lot of time and patience. But in accepting our differences, and learning to work together as a team we can find much of what is truly enjoyable about being in a family.

The amount of patience needed to be a good parent is phenomenal. It is natural for children to constantly challenge their parents. It is a struggle for parents to be patient when they are constantly being challenged, are overwhelmed with other responsibilities, and are frequently in a state of fatigue. There's good reason why it is said that parenting is the most difficult of all jobs!

However, it is also one of the most rewarding. When we are able to keep our "eyes on the prize"—to realize that there is nothing more important in our lives than loving our children and helping them grow up to be happy, secure, kind, and responsible adults, it becomes a little easier to cope. There will still be times when we lose our patience. But we can get it back again. There may even be times when we find ourselves apologizing to our children several times in a single day for being impatient with them. Fortunately, our children are very forgiving. They may not have much patience for tying their shoes or waiting for their turn, but the amount of tolerance they have for a parent whose heart is in the right place, and who is trying to do her best, is impressive.

We want our children to develop the capacity to calmly accept and successfully cope with whatever aggravations they encounter in their lives. By finding—and holding on to—the serenity within ourselves that we need to be patient with our children, we can create a home in which the daily struggles of life may be challenging but are not overwhelming. Such a home, where tolerance for others makes it possible for us to enjoy each other in small but important ways even in the midst of the daily rush, will give our children an example to aspire to, and the strength they will need to draw on for the rest of their lives.

If children live with praise, they learn appreciation

Think of praise as a way of expressing your love. Your words of praise encourage your children and make them feel deeply appreciated and valued. Praise nurtures their developing sense of self and helps them learn how to appreciate who they are, as well as who they're becoming.

Praising our children for their attempts as well as their achievements is one of our most important jobs as parents. We should feel free to give our praise generously: there's no such thing as too much praise when it comes to bolstering a child's emerging sense of self. When we recognize and draw attention to their inherent value, we are helping our children build a storehouse of confidence that they can draw on when we're not around or when times get tough. It's not overstating the case to say that the praise and appreciation we lavish on our children now could last them a lifetime.

When we praise our children, we also provide them with a model for how to notice and express their appreciation of others and the world around them. This will help them to create healthy relationships and become the kind of people who enjoy life, bringing a positive attitude to the situations and people they encounter. Praise prepares them to be a more pleasant person for others to be around.

Deserving Praise

When children are praised they learn the true meaning of appreciation, and it touches their sense of inherent worth and dignity. Every child deserves to feel this way, and it is our job as parents to encourage its flowering.

Praise shouldn't always need to be earned, and children shouldn't have to prove themselves in order to be appreciated. As parents, one of our challenges is to pay close attention to the subtle nuances of our children's unique personalities and to praise them for the qualities we want to encourage as they mature.

At a family picnic, a few preadolescent children are playing badminton together, volleying the birdie back and forth, diving wildly, swinging and missing, and just having fun. Ryan, one of the twelve-year-old boys, gives his racket to his five-year-old sister and then lifts her onto his shoulders, so she, too, can play. She is thrilled to be included with the big kids and she even hits the birdie now and then.

When the children break for soda, Ryan's mother says to him quietly, "You're really a sweet brother to include your sister." Ryan shrugs and runs off with the other kids, but there is a shy smile on his face he can't quite hide. He knows his mother appreciates his kindness toward his sister. It makes him feel good about himself in a fundamental way, and leaves him with the feeling that his goodness is recognized and valued.

Even on their worst days, there will always be something positive about our children we can choose to notice and praise, especially if we can remember to always give them the benefit of the doubt.

Four-year-old Frederick and his little brother, Joseph, who is not yet two, are playing in their bedroom. Suddenly the peaceful sounds of play are shattered by a flurry of crying and screaming. Mom comes to the door of their room, and says, "What happened?"

"Joey took my truck!" says Freddy, tearfully. He is holding a metal tow truck as high as he can above his head, while little Joey swings at him, trying to reach it.

This time Mom decides to skip the questions about who had what first, and who took what from whom. Instead, she observes, "You don't want Joey to play with your truck."

"No, he's too little," says Freddy emphatically. "He might hurt himself," he adds, a little more softly.

Mom notices that Freddy has a point. The tow truck is made of metal, and is really made for an older child. "I think it's nice that you're concerned about your little brother," she says. "Do you have another toy you think he would like to play with, that might be better for him?"

Freddy looks around the room and sees a big wooden

truck. He hands the tow truck to his mother, who discreetly moves it out of sight. "I think he might like this one," he says, handing the wooden truck to his brother. Joey smiles and begins to play with the wooden truck, and Freddy returns to his own activity, relieved that his tow truck has been removed from circulation, and proud—if perhaps a bit confused—by the role of protective big brother he has just been assigned.

Freddy's claim to have been concerned about his little brother's safety may or may not have been the real reason he wasn't letting him play with the truck. But it doesn't really matter: the point is that he has had the positive experience of being seen as a good big brother and a problem-solver, and he has been able to help in resolving a distressing situation. His mother has been willing to believe that he is doing his best, and this is important to Freddy, too. By letting our children know that we believe in them and expect the best of them we provide an environment in which they can not only meet but surpass their own expectations of themselves.

Teaching Values Through Praise

When we praise our children for some things more than others, we are teaching them what is important to us. Unfortunately, in our consumer society, kids are barraged with the message that personal worth and value are determined by the amount and type of material possessions we own. It's important to find ways to balance the consumer-oriented values to which our children are constantly exposed with our own, less materialistic, values. We can start by letting our children know we love them first and foremost for being who they are.

We can work at actively countering the sometimes subtle, sometimes flagrant, messages our children are exposed to daily. Starting at an early age, we can help them notice the fact that they are surrounded by advertising and other cultural messages that are designed to make them think they need all kinds of things they don't. We can point out that although these messages imply that possessions can bring happiness, friendship, and love, they really can't. Teaching them a healthy skepticism toward advertising and how to tell the difference between wanting and needing something will help them become wiser consumers as well as happier, more well-balanced human beings.

When we show our children that we appreciate them for who they are, we are also teaching them how to make sound judgments about the people they encounter in their lives. When a new boy, Timothy, entered Jake's fifth-grade classroom, he made quite an impression on all the kids. He had lived abroad with his family, spoke several languages, and was a very good athlete. Word quickly spread that he had a big house with all the newest video games, a giant-screen TV, and a pool table. All the boys wanted to play with him at his house.

However, when Jake was invited, he found that Timothy was domineering, difficult, and sometimes just plain mean. After his father picked him up from Timothy's house, Jake sat silently on the ride home.

"What did you two do all afternoon? Did you have fun?" his dad asked.

Jake began to describe their activities, and then started complaining about how Timothy always had to have his way, needed to win every game, and didn't play fair.

Jake's dad listened attentively for a while. When there was a pause, he asked, "So what did you think about the way Tim acted?"

"I didn't like it," Jake said emphatically.

"Hmm. What didn't you like?" Dad asked.

"He can have a house full of great stuff but I still don't want to play with him!" Jake burst out.

Jake's father let his son's words sink in, then said, "I'm proud of you, Jake, for knowing that it's the person, not how many nice things they have, that's important."

Dad is supporting Jake's decision to evaluate the person rather than his possessions. Simple conversations like these, squeezed into odd moments of our busy days, provide opportunities to affirm the positive values our children are developing and make sense of our own values to them, showing them how these values can be translated into the situations presented by everyday living.

The Importance of Sincerity

It's important to praise our children, but it's even more important to be sincere in our praise. The way parents behave on the sidelines of the athletic field often tells a lot about what qualities they value. Some parents make it clear by the way they behave that to them, winning is everything.

Nine-year-old Robby has gone out for Little League. He's not a great athlete, but he enjoys playing and he's learning some important physical as well as social skills through his participation in the sport. Most of the time he tries hard and does reasonably well. However, one day during a game against another team, his heart doesn't seem to be in it. Robby's mother is standing on the sidelines, frantically screaming for his team to win. Her cheering is particularly intense whenever Robby is up at bat or a ball is coming his way in the outfield. The more she screams, the more he seems to fumble and falter.

After the game, which his team loses, his mother says, "It's all right, you know. You tried," but after the way she behaved throughout the game, and because of her tone of voice, Robby knows she doesn't really mean it.

There will always be times when we will be disappointed in our children, and there is no point in trying to hide our feelings. However, what is most important is how our children feel about their own efforts. When things don't go well, and kids know it, we need to take it easy on our own disappointment. What Robby needs is a big hug and reassurance from his mom that she's on his side, no matter who wins. We have to remember that what's important is that our kids are learning the rules of good sportsmanship, working together as a team, giving their best effort, and having fun. After all, it is not our aspirations for our children that will determine their lives, but rather their own goals and dreams for themselves.

We provide a better example for our kids when our feelings and our actions match as closely as possible. This is a somewhat complicated matter, however. On the one hand, we want our children to say what they mean, and mean what they say, at least most of the time. On the other hand, we want them to develop a sense of when total honesty is called for, and when certain things are better left unsaid. We don't want our children to be phony, but we do want them to be polite and considerate of others' feelings. And while it's important to teach them good manners and the formalities of please and thank-you, we want to do more than just teach them to say the right words. We want them to genuinely appreciate the thoughtfulness and generosity of others. This is not an easy job, but one of the best ways we can tackle it is by providing our children with a model of behavior that strikes a balance between kindness and frankness, honesty and diplomacy, showing them through our own actions how to negotiate these delicate but important social interactions.

Teaching Kids to Appreciate Themselves

There's a difference between being appreciated by others and by oneself, although both are important. We want our children to become emotionally mature, and to learn how to give themselves the support and encouragement they need as they become more independent. If they can appreciate themselves, they will have a source of emotional nourishment that is always available. Of course, this learning starts when they're very young.

As Mom is picking up her four-year-old daughter from nursery school she stops to speak briefly with the teacher. The girl interrupts them to show her mother the puzzle she has put together.

Admiring her work, Mom says, "I'm proud of you. That's such a good job."

The teacher gently adds, "Aren't you proud of yourself for doing that?"

The child beams. Now she has received praise from others and encouragement to appreciate herself as well.

The Limits of Praise

Praise should not be used as a substitute for love and attention. We need to be aware that when our children constantly seek out and demand praise—"Look at me, see how good I can do this?"—in effect they are saying,

"Please notice me and tell me I'm okay." When children demand this kind of attention frequently, they may be looking for reassurance that they are loved and supported, which is a more basic need than the need to be appreciated for one's accomplishments. If this is the case, merely heaping on the praise will not meet the need.

Four-year-old Joshua is drawing on a pad on the floor while his mother has a cup of coffee at the kitchen table.

"See what I'm making?" Joshua asks his mom, holding up the very beginnings of a drawing.

Mom looks at the paper and says, "That's a good start. What comes next?"

Joshua ignores her question, gathers up his paper and crayons and approaches his mother, "Can I sit on your lap?" he asks.

Mom moves her coffee cup aside and makes room for Josh to climb up. She knows her son needs to be held more than he needs artistic encouragement. More importantly, he knows what he needs and is not afraid to ask for it.

Some children need more attention than others. There is a great deal of individual difference in this area: some children require a lot of hand-holding and snuggling, while others are content to wave happily to their parents from a distance. For those kids who need a great deal of attention, praise and appreciation are not enough. They need their parents' focused attention and demonstrative affection in order to feel confident that they are loved.

When there are changes in the household—divorce, the illness or death of a parent, a move to a new location, or the loss of a parent's job—most children will temporarily need more attention and nurturing. In such times, it's vital to stay close to children and talk about what's happening. By helping them to share their feelings and worries, we give them the chance to get extra attention in a way that can be comforting, healing, and reassuring.

The Art of Appreciation

We want our children to learn how to receive praise as well as give it. When they grow up surrounded by praise, they learn to accept it gracefully and with gratitude, rather than with embarrassment, denial, or self-aggrandizement.

When we appreciate and praise our children, we teach them to appreciate and celebrate the world around them. Taking the time and making the effort to find the good in each day will make our children's lives, and their memories of their childhood, much happier.

If children live with acceptance, they learn to love

We use the word "love" to describe the most dynamic and vital human experience there is. What we call love is bigger than anything we can say about it. And most people would agree that there is nothing more important in life than to love and be loved.

When we wholeheartedly love our children and accept them unconditionally, they thrive. Love is the soil in which our children grow, the sunlight that determines their direction, the water that nourishes their growth.

Children need love from the moment they are born—and even before that. Newborns are totally dependent on our warmth, affection, and loving attention. Our active caring nurtures their feelings of being wanted and belonging. As children mature, they continue to rely on us to show them we love them. They best understand our love through our kind and caring actions. Our total acceptance of them is the wellspring of our love.

While it is imperative for our children to feel loved, love is a fundamental human need that we never outgrow. As adults, we still want to be wanted. We still need human connection, closeness, affection, and a warm touch. We all want to be accepted for being who we are, and to have friends with whom we feel we belong.

Our children know they are wanted and loved when we treat them kindly, and when we accompany loving actions with loving words and nurturing touch. It is not enough to say "I love you." In working with parents, I often talk about the three A's of love: acceptance, affection, and appreciation. Our children need to live in an atmosphere where they feel confident that they will always be accepted and loved despite their shortcomings. When they are loved in this way, they will be able to mature in their ability to love others.

Unconditional Acceptance Teaches Love

The root of the word acceptance is "to bring to ourselves"—to receive. When we are accepting, we "bring to ourselves" repeatedly. This is exactly how we teach our children they are wanted and loved. We convey our love with smiles, hugs, kisses, and pats, with the warmth of our affection, day in and day out, through all the years of childhood and into their adulthood.

When we accept our children unconditionally we let go of any inclination we may have to want to change their inner selves, who they are. In order to do this, we may have to give up some of our oldest and fondest dreams. The mother whose daughter prefers reading to ballet and the father whose son decides he likes chemistry better than basketball are faced with a choice about which is more important: living out their dreams through their children or providing their kids with the emotional support and acceptance they need to find and pursue their own dreams. Seen this way, the choice should be clear, and when we make room for our children's hopes to unfold, we make our own world much bigger and richer, too.

We also need to let our children know that achievements or compliance with our requests are not prerequisites for being loved. Love should always be freely given, not offered as a reward for good behavior. We should never threaten to withhold or withdraw our love, or set conditions for it by saying "I won't love you if . . . " or "I'll love you when. . . . " Some parents are concerned that if they unconditionally accept their children, they will "never have anything to strive toward." But children need to strive toward goals and achievements, not the fundamental right to be accepted and loved by their parents.

However, accepting our children unconditionally does not mean tolerating inappropriate or irresponsible behavior. We can accept our kids while rejecting their unacceptable behaviors and maintaining rules and limits.

Six-year-old Jason has left his bicycle in the driveway—again. His father has repeatedly asked him to put it on the porch, explaining that he's afraid that one day he may run over it by accident. But Jason keeps forgetting. Finally, one night the inevitable happens, and Dad feels the dreaded crunch under his wheels.

He's angry when he walks through the front door, but with an effort he keeps his temper. Unaware of what has happened, Jason runs up to greet his father with a hug.

Dad bends down to meet his son and swoops him up. "I want to show you something," he says in a serious tone. He carries Jason to the window, where he can see the damaged bicycle.

"Oh no!" Jason cries as he realizes what has happened. He holds on tighter to his father's neck, and buries his face in his shoulder.

"You left your bike in the driveway," Dad states simply. Jason nods his head. His father continues to hold him, adding "This is what I was afraid might happen." Dad puts Jason back on his feet. He looks his son directly in the eyes and says, "You understand that it may be ruined?" The boy nods tearfully. "Let's go take a closer look at it," Dad says, adding, "Maybe we'll be able to fix it." The message Dad is giving Jason is, "Even if I don't always love what you do, I still love you and will help and support you."

Showing Them We Care

While children need to be told they are loved, they need even more to be assured, through hugs, kisses, gentle pats, and snuggling, that the words we speak are genuine. The need to be touched is perhaps one of the most fundamental, most universal, and most powerful needs in our lives, as important for the newborn baby as it is for his grandparents. In fact, recent research has confirmed what people have long known intuitively: that there is a healing power in loving touch. After any needed first aid, the warmth of a loving touch can send a message of support to our body's healing response.

Our children are entitled to the comfort of our touch. Sitting in the circle of Mom or Dad's arms can calm a child in need of comforting, whether it's because his knees are skinned or his feelings have been hurt. Sometimes even a warm hug or a gentle pat can help soothe and restore.

The importance of demonstrating the affection we feel for our children cannot be overstated. In one of my parenting groups, a mother confessed "I've been feeling guilty because I didn't think I loved my little boy enough. But maybe I should be saying I don't express my love enough."

Some parents need help learning how to provide the affection their children need. One mother described her childhood in a family that was quite distant and reserved. Her parents loved her, but they didn't express their love. When she became a mother, she continued this family pattern. She loved her two-year-old daughter very much, yet it wasn't in her nature to be demonstrative.

Because this mother was sensitive to her daughter's needs, she was determined to break the cycle and to learn how to express the love she felt. She made a conscious effort to pick her daughter up more frequently, snuggle closely while reading to her, and give her hugs while helping her on and off the swing. She found dozens of opportunities every day to give her daughter the affection she had never received from her parents. When she returned to the parenting class after a couple of weeks of practicing this, she reported, "You know, I started out doing this for her, but now I realize it's important for me, too."

Demonstrative affection is vital for all children. They need the physical assurance that goes with "I love you." The repetition of our endearments and the constancy of our affection allows them to fully experience our love, and should never be withheld.

A Loving Example

The way Mom and Dad treat each other and show how they care for one another can provide a powerful model of acceptance and love in family life. Children are keen observers, learning about marriage by watching their parents. The example we provide for our children in our everyday interactions often becomes a template for the relationships our children will have when they marry. In fact, the way we treat our spouses sets a pattern for our children's lives that may be one of the most influential factors for their future success, personal fulfillment, and happiness. It affects the kind of people they will be attracted to and provides a model for the types of relationships they will create in their own families, for better or worse.

So, while there is no magic recipe for a happy marriage, we must do our best to provide a loving example. A mature and healthy relationship involves a balance in giving and receiving. It involves accepting each other's strengths and weaknesses, as well as the ability to give tenderness, empathy, and compassion. Our children see how we care for and nurture each other, and they also see when we fail to do so. When we respect and support one another and treat each other with warmth and affection—sharing interests and values while accepting individual differences—we give them a model for how to build and sustain a happy marriage.

A Foundation to Build On

Children who are secure about being accepted and loved have the inner strength they need to pursue their goals and extend themselves to others. And children who are surrounded with the warmth and caring, the acceptance and love they need, learn how to love themselves. When they grow up knowing that they deserve love and expecting that they will be loved, they will be able to give as well as receive love and sustain loving relationships. Whatever else they do in their lives, surely there is nothing more important than this.

If children live with approval, they learn to like themselves

P arental attitudes shape children. By the way we express our approval or disapproval of our kids, and by the things we choose to encourage, we teach them a lot about our own values. At the same time, we can let them know what we like and want to see more of in their developing character and personality, as well as in their behavior.

If we're too busy to pay attention or if we take our children for granted, we miss the chance to nurture the qualities and behaviors we'd like them to develop. It's the little things our children do that help create the kind of people they will become: these "little things" are precisely the things we need to applaud.

Dad comes in from working in the yard one afternoon, and seven-year-old Stephen meets him at the door. He holds his finger to his lips and solemnly whispers, "Shh, Mom is taking a nap."

"Thanks for being so considerate," Dad whispers back, giving Stephen a hug.

We don't have to take a lot of time to make the most of these moments. Indeed, a simple phrase or gesture of appreciation will often do the trick. Mom's been working at her desk when she realizes the house is unusually quiet. She peeks into Rebecca's room and finds her five-year-old daughter quietly rocking her doll in her toy cradle.

Rebecca looks up and smiles. Mom blows her a kiss and gives her a thumbs-up. As she returns to her desk, Mom thinks how pleased she is that Rebecca is being such a sweet "mommy" to her doll. She also likes the fact that Rebecca is learning to play independently and feels good about being by herself.

These are the moments we don't want to miss, but in the hurry and scurry of everyday life it's not always easy to remember to acknowledge them. We need to constantly remind ourselves how important it is to make these moments count.

Teaching Values, Building Self-Esteem

We can think of our approval as a way of affirming our child's emerging self, helping him build a positive self-image and healthy self-esteem. The more we notice and draw attention to what's right about our kids, the more we reinforce the budding qualities we want them to develop.

Dad says, "You were really a good helper today when Grandma was here. I liked the way you helped her get up from the sofa."

"You did?" asks eight-year-old Brad, surprised. He didn't know Dad had even noticed. In fact, he hadn't thought about it himself. By drawing attention to his son's kind action, Dad is letting him know that kindness and consideration toward others are important to him. This is the way family values are taught and passed from one generation to the next.

Sometimes by the things we choose to notice, we teach our children to appreciate qualities in themselves that they might otherwise be unaware of. Seven-year-old Amanda has learned a new way to make bracelets out of embroidery thread. All her girlfriends love her new bracelet, so Amanda begins making them for her friends, selecting just the right colors for each girl.

Amanda's mom could express her approval for various aspects of this project. She might focus on Amanda's artistic ability by saying, "Your bracelets are beautiful. You have a wonderful sense of color." Or she might focus on their commercial potential: "These bracelets are great! I bet you could sell them at the craft show." This time, Mom chooses to focus on Amanda's generosity. "How thoughtful of you to make a special bracelet for each of your friends!" she says. In her choice of emphasis, Mom does more than simply approve of Amanda's hobby. She lets her know that she is especially proud of her generosity and thoughtfulness, and paves the way for Amanda to recognize and value the same qualities in herself.

Of course, different families have different values and they express their approval accordingly. Our ability to influence what our children come to value and like about themselves is a major way we can contribute both to their developing identities and to their emerging morality.

Learning to Live With Agreements

Every household operates with a set of many specific as well as general agreements that facilitate the flow of everyday living within the family. From dinnertime protocol to the level of neatness required in living areas to bedtime rituals, parents and children share innumerable assumptions which make it easier to coexist as a family. Such agreements are the glue that hold things together in a family, helping kids and parents to meet each other's expectations.

Some family rules are nonnegotiable, such as the ones required for safety—wearing seat belts in the car, elbow and knee pads for roller-blading, a hat when it's cold outside. Others may be designed to promote efficiency or general order, and are more likely to be flexible—dishes go into the dishwasher right after dinner, toys get put away before we go out, no TV before homework is done. The more children are included in the process of creating and negotiating these agreements, the more likely they are to cooperate, and the better they will accept their parents' disapproval when they don't.

Having house rules gives children a comforting sense of predictability and makes it easier for them to understand what is expected of them. They know that when they follow the rules of the house, they are meeting with our approval, even when it is unstated. Even when parents are divorced, and the children have to learn and comply with two different sets of house rules, having these guidelines makes life easier for them. It's amazing how well children understand the complicated dynamics involved in negotiating rules and how easily they learn to translate them into their own terms. When Billy says to a friend, "I'll ask my mother. If she says, 'We'll see,' we're on. If she says, 'Let's ask your dad,' forget it," he shows how well he understands the implicit dynamics that prevail in his home.

Children ask for our approval for dozens of activities on a daily basis. Some are simple requests for permission with the assumption of acceptance. When Artie yells from the back door, "Mom! I'm going next door to see the new puppy, okay?" and Mom hears the screen door slam before she has a chance to answer, she knows he is complying with the rule that she wants to know his whereabouts, even if he's only going next door.

Other requests are more complicated, requiring the ability to negotiate a transaction between parent and child. One Saturday afternoon eleven-year-old Marianne is invited to go to the movies with a friend. But she hasn't cleaned up her room all week, and it's a house rule that there are no play dates on the weekend unless the children's rooms are clean. Marianne doesn't have time to do it now, but she really wants to accept the invitation.

Mom and Marianne sit down to discuss a compromise solution. They agree that Marianne will be allowed to go to the movies this time. But she has to spend the next fifteen minutes beginning the job of cleaning her room, and she must promise to finish the task when she gets home. They also talk about why it's a good idea to keep up with regular tasks and not always leave them until the last possible moment. Marianne is allowed to go to the movies with her friend, but this situation has helped her to realize that her habit of procrastinating is not a good one.

If children learn to negotiate and live up to their agreements when they're young, the more complex situations of adolescence will be easier to handle. When your teenager says, "I'm going out with the guys after school, so I'll be late," without putting him through the third degree, you need to find out which guys, where they're going, how they're getting there, and what is meant by "late."

It's best to start out by approving of your child's approach to the situation, if you can. "I'm glad you thought to bring this up" sets a positive tone and helps him to see his request for approval as a form of consideration. It also tacitly expresses the notion that the parent/child relationship is a collaborative one, with room for both the child's growing need for independence and the parent's continuing need to protect him from harm. This allows him to see himself in a new light as he outlines his plans. He knows his parents will expect him to follow the plan they agree on, and unless the relationship has become one of open hostility, most children will try, even during the difficult teenage years, to please their parents most of the time.

Learning how to honor agreements and live within the family structure prepares children to fit in with the larger communities of school and work. Ultimately it prepares them to take their place within the structure of society. Through their experience in the home, our children come to understand that laws are basically agreements people have made that help them get things done or provide safety and protection for everyone. They realize that agreements are what make the world go around—whether between individuals or between nations.

Values They Can Hold Onto

When we speak about approval and disapproval, we are talking about making value judgments: right/wrong, good/bad, better/worse. Even when we don't state our feelings explicitly, our children are experts at knowing what we approve of as well as what we don't. This doesn't mean that their behavior will always reflect this knowledge. As they mature, our kids will inevitably develop their own standards and values, and they may not always be the same as ours. While this may be disappointing at times, if our children grow up to be responsible human beings who make their decisions conscientiously and in good faith, we should be pleased whether or not we agree with every specific decision they make.

Particularly during the teenage years, peer pressure can become a major influence in their lives. We cannot be with our children all the time, and we cannot make them do the right thing. That is why it is so important that the messages we give them about making ethical decisions as they are growing up are clear and strong, without being so rigid that they will inevitably lead to rebellion. Then when it comes time for them to choose, our children will have a strong foundation to draw upon, and they will want to do what is right.

In this regard, the example of our own behavior is extremely important. We can tell our children that lying is wrong and punish them when they lie to us, but what are they to think if they hear us call in sick to work so we can go to a baseball game? If we want our children to maintain a high standard of ethical behavior, we will have to show them by our own example how to do so, even if it is sometimes inconvenient.

We want our children to like themselves and develop a positive self-image that is independent of others' approval or disapproval. We want them to be able to evaluate their own actions and have the inner strength to act accordingly.

Twelve-year-old Bruce often went to the neighborhood grocery store, sometimes on an errand for his mother, other times to buy himself a soda or a snack. Bruce knew that other kids were stealing from the store, especially when one clerk, who didn't seem to care, was on duty.

One day, as he entered the store Bruce had an urge for a snack, but he only had enough money for the milk and eggs his mom wanted. He knew it would be simple to swipe something: the "easy" clerk was on, and was deeply involved in reading a magazine.

Bruce decided not to take advantage of the situation. Although he knew his parents would have seriously disapproved of his stealing, he also knew he probably wouldn't get caught. So the thought of their disapproval may have slowed him down, but it isn't what stopped him. At twelve years of age, Bruce had internalized the rule that stealing is wrong, and he liked himself well enough to want to do what was right, even though the circumstances to do wrong were tempting. For his own peace of mind and to feel good about himself, Bruce resisted the temptation to steal.

Our endorsement of specific behaviors can only go so far. We need to support our children's developing self-esteem so they can like themselves on their own terms as well as hold firm to what they know is right when outside pressures inevitably challenge them.

Teaching Our Children to Like Themselves

When asked what they want for their children, most parents will answer, "I just want them to be happy." Although liking oneself doesn't automatically lead to happiness, it does seem to be an essential ingredient. Children who like themselves tend to be more self-confident without being egotistical. They develop warmer and more stable relationships and, as adults, are more likely to have children who like themselves.

Five-year-old Laurel is playing dress-up, entertaining her grandma. Every time she emerges from her imaginary dressing room, otherwise known as her toy closet, Grandma claps and asks her about the new outfit.

"And where will you go in this one?" she wants to know.

With all the dignity she can muster, tottering in her mother's high heels, Laurel answers, "To the ball."

"And will the prince fall in love with you?" Grandma asks.

Laurel looks at her grandmother, furrowing her brow deep in five-year-old thought. "Maybe," she replies, as if it's the least of her concerns. Then she wraps her arms around herself in a hug and runs toward Grandma to collapse in her lap amidst uncontrollable giggles. It seems that the prince's approval is not the critical issue. Laurel is clearly happy with herself. Her laughter is contagious and Grandma joins in, glad in the knowledge that this grandchild is going to be just fine.

As parents, the agreements we make with our children reflect what is important to us. They shape our expectations of our children, and help them learn how to tell right from wrong and good from bad. We make it easier for our children to gain our approval when we have realistic expectations of them, when we are firm but flexible, and when we create with them a family setting in which their contributions are respected and integrated into family life. In such a supportive and nurturing environment, they are free to blossom into their own best selves, and are given a very important gift: the knowledge that they are loved and valued for their own special talents. This understanding provides them with the best possible basis for growing into adults with a healthy respect for their own worthiness.

If children live with recognition, they learn it is good to have a goal

D o you ever tape a note to yourself on your alarm clock, bathroom mirror, or front door? Have you found, like the rest of us, that you get so used to the note being there that you no longer see it? This is one reason why the warning on refrigerator doors, "Opening this door may be hazardous to your health" doesn't work. We stop paying attention.

In a similar way, sometimes we stop seeing our children. We get so caught up in juggling all the myriad demands in our lives that we forget to focus on our kids. We take them to school, make dinner for them, oversee their activities, but we fail to stop and have a real conversation with them.

The word recognition means "to know again"—to see anew. Children grow and change so quickly. It seems that in just a few days a baby can change into a toddler and a youngster into a teenager. Our children grow up right under our noses, and sometimes we are so busy we miss steps in the process. We need to regularly make the effort to know them again, to see them as if for the first time.

Recognizing our children isn't hard. It's simply a matter of taking the time to pay attention. Our attention in itself nurtures and comforts, energizes and encourages them.

While walking through the park one autumn day, four-year-old Elyssa tugs on her mother's sleeve and says, "Can we go over there? I want to get some of those big leaves."

"But sweetie, the grass is wet and you've already picked up a lot of leaves," Mom replies.

"But I don't have that kind of leaf, and I need it for my collection," Elyssa says insistently.

Mom looks down at her daughter in surprise. She had noticed that Elyssa was picking up leaves, but she hadn't given it any thought. She had no idea Elyssa was making a collection; in fact, she didn't know that Elyssa even knew what a collection was. Mom recognizes that creating and following through on a project of her own is indication of her daughter's budding independence. She stops, admires the bunch of leaves in Elyssa's hand, and watches her run across the grass to an old oak tree. On the way home they talk about the names of the various types of trees and how each leaf has its own color and shape.

If we take the time to try to truly see our children—to listen to what they say, watch what they do, find out how they're feeling—it will be much easier for us to appreciate their struggles and successes as they learn how to work toward a goal. This knowledge will help us to determine when to let them labor by themselves and when to lend a hand to help them.

Step by Step

From the first time we opt not to hand the baby a toy and instead let her figure out a way to creep over, scoot around, or roll over to reach it, we are letting her know that it's good to have a goal. We recognize her effort when we applaud her attempts to reach the toy, and share in her delight when she finally holds it in her hand.

When children are a little older, setting and accomplishing goals helps them develop confidence and a "can-do" attitude. As parents, we can help our children be clear about their goals and make sure they're attainable. We can provide a reality check, helping them balance their flights of imagination with down-to-earth advice. And while they work to achieve their goals, we can be there to offer encouragement and support.

For anyone, young or old, the best way to start working toward a goal is to first define exactly what it is we want to accomplish. The next step is to identify what needs to be done, by breaking the project into small steps. We offer our children a great service when we help them do this. As they work their way through the steps, they learn how doing "A" first allows "B" to happen, thus making "C" possible, and they see that ultimately, once all the steps have been taken, the goal is met.

This may sound rather basic, but it's astonishing how few of us organize ourselves by first defining the steps we need to take to meet our goals. More often, we launch into projects headlong, without taking the time to plan our efforts. With this approach it's easy to become scattered, overwhelmed, or unclear about our direction, and then to lose focus and momentum. This is not a good model for our kids. We provide our children with a better example when we start by mapping out a strategy and staying with the project, sharing our progress along the way and celebrating our success when we finish the job. Whether we're painting the house, planting a garden, or sewing a quilt, our children learn from observing the way we plan and carry out projects, as well as those projects we choose to do.

The old saying about the journey being as important as the destination may not only help us get organized to attain our goals, but can also help us remember to recognize and honor our children's faltering first steps as they struggle to accomplish theirs.

Five-year-old Jacqueline wants to surprise her parents by making their bed for them. With a good bit of running around the bedroom, she manages to pull the bedcover up most of the way.

Mom and Dad thank her, saying, "Nice job! You're such a big help." As Jacqueline is happily running outside to play, Dad moves toward the bed, reaching his hand out to straighten a corner of the bedspread.

"Don't you touch that bed!" Mom laughingly warns. "Jacqueline's work needs to be recognized and accepted as it is. Let's not ruin it."

"You're right," Dad agrees. He realizes that appreciating his daughter's effort is more important than a perfectly made bed.

Practice, Practice, Practice

Some children have no trouble seeing the relationship between the efforts they make, and the outcome. At an early age, they understand that the more they practice— playing the piano, doing gymnastics, batting, or whatever they're interested in—the better they'll become at it. For other kids, this connection is not so obvious: they will ask someone whose accomplishments they admire with genuine astonishment, "How did you get so good?" They don't understand that their actions can have a cumulative effect. To them, successful results seem almost magical.

By showing our children how their actions build on each other, we can help them realize that they don't need magic to achieve a goal or to become accomplished. Elizabeth and Clara, both twelve, were planning to go to a summer camp for field hockey. They both knew they would be out on the field all day for two full weeks. Clara began working out a month before camp began, slowly building up her stamina, until she was running about three miles every morning. Elizabeth figured she would adjust to the intensity of the schedule when she got to camp.

Elizabeth's mom was concerned that her daughter might be in for a rude awakening. She knew Elizabeth wouldn't want to be told what to do. So instead she decided to help her daughter look ahead by asking her a couple of leading questions: "How many hours a day will you be playing?" and "Did the camp make any suggestions about how to prepare?" She never said, "You have to begin training," or acted as if she knew better than her daughter. Instead, she helped guide Elizabeth through the process of thinking ahead for herself. Together they discussed what to expect and what Elizabeth could do to prepare herself. With her mom's timely but subtle intervention, Elizabeth decided she should start a training program to get into shape.

Saving Money for a Goal

Receiving an allowance is often the first chance a child has to learn about "the value of a dollar"—how much various things cost, and how to develop good saving habits and set aside money for a specific goal. When they are put in charge of their own money, children quickly learn that if they forego spending their money on candy this week, they may be able to buy something really special for themselves later on—in-line skates, a computer game, a doll, or a bicycle. It's also one way children can assert their independence and exercise greater decision-making power. When a certain toy or video game is their heart's desire, but Mom and Dad don't want to buy it for them, that doesn't have to be the final word. Having an allowance gives children a greater voice, and can help minimize power struggles over how to spend money.

There are various ideas about what an allowance should represent. In some families, children earn their allowance by completing certain agreed-upon household tasks. In others, the allowance is unrelated to specific tasks, but children can earn extra money by taking on additional projects. My own view is that an allowance should not be seen as a child's payment for helping with the daily tasks needed to make a household run smoothly, like setting or clearing the table, taking out the trash, or feeding the dog. We want our children to recognize that as family members they need to do their part to help out around the house. Rather, an allowance should be seen as a way of sharing the family income, one way of recognizing that the child is an important, participating member of the family.

Twelve-year-old Sam had been saving his allowance for months with the goal of buying a skateboard by spring. His parents did not consider a skateboard to be a basic need, so they told Sam they thought he could use his own money to buy one. Sam reluctantly agreed it was a "want" and not a "need." But when April rolled around and he was still short about twenty dollars, he became frustrated.

"You've done a great job saving your money over the winter. What could you do now to earn the rest of the amount you need?" Sam's father asked.

"Well, it's a little too early for yard work," Sam answered, discouraged.

"Yes, but the timing is perfect for washing cars. Get all the winter dirt and grime off," Dad pointed out.

Sam brightened, "Yeah! Get ready for spring." So Sam put some flyers around his neighborhood and got about a half dozen cars to wash. He even hired his younger brother to help him.

Sam's dad supported him in his goal to buy the skateboard by recognizing how much he'd already accomplished and helping him to identify the next step toward his goal. Through this experience, Sam learned about saving and earning money: perhaps even more importantly, he also learned not to give up on his goal, but to persist until he had found a way to achieve it.

Helping Them Toward Their Goals

We want our children to have an optimistic, confident viewpoint about their personal dreams and goals. We know there will be discouraging moments, but by recognizing each of the steps along the way, and encouraging them to persist in the face of frustration, we can help them maintain a positive attitude and achieve the goals they have set for themselves.

There are opportunities to recognize children, and to encourage their optimism, everywhere we turn. One afternoon, I answered the doorbell. Outside my door I saw four shining faces beaming up at me. It was a neighbor's eight-year-old daughter and three of her friends. Each of them was holding a colorful chain of yarn with a clay ball attached to one end and bright beads to the other. "We made them! Everybody needs one, and they're only fifty cents," they said. Their enthusiasm was irresistible. I bought two.

"They" now hang in my breakfast room window. The morning sun glances off the glass beads, brightening their beautiful colors. What are they? What are they for? I don't know. I bought them because I wanted to encourage the entrepreneurial spirit of these children, to let them know that it is good to have a goal. And I keep them in my breakfast room because looking at them makes me smile, and encourages me, too.

If children live with sharing, they learn generosity

L iving in a family is about sharing ourselves with others: our time, our space, and our energy. Our children learn to share with others when they have the experience of cooperating and compromising within the family, whether it's over the use of the one bathroom in the house, the toys, the car, or limited financial resources. When we share gracefully with others and with our children, we show them how to be generous. True generosity cannot be taught, but we can provide our children with a model of unselfish giving that we hope they will choose to follow.

I often hear parents tell their young children they "have to" share. We may think this is teaching them how to share, but all it's really teaching them is to do what we say. They are not learning anything about the spirit of generosity that moves us to share with others.

Where Sharing Starts

L et's face it. Part of the reason we want our children to share is that we don't want others to see them as being selfish. However, it's very important to keep in mind the limitations presented by their young age. The process of becoming unselfish depends in large part on the slow and gradual development of the cognitive abilities that allow a child to take into account the feelings and needs of others. Very young children are not ready to share because they literally cannot put themselves in another's place. The ability to see the world through someone else's eyes is a long-term process that continues to unfold until our children are well into adulthood.

Way back in the cradle the infant "owns" everything in the universe, including Mom and Dad. In fact, the newborn infant cannot even differentiate himself from his parents. A major developmental milestone is reached when he is able to recognize his mother as a separate being.

Because they are not able to really understand anyone's viewpoint but their own, it's natural for little children to be selfish. They want it all, and they want it now. So what if your little girl or boy shows it? So do millions of other toddlers around the planet. It is part of our job as parents to gradually teach them about unselfishness, one small step at a time.

It's best to start with sharing that doesn't involve personal sacrifice. You can help this process along very early on, even with a toddler in the high chair, by emphasizing certain key words and introducing the concept of sharing as dividing a whole into parts. "We share the carrots: you get some, I get some." Or "Mommy gets a cookie, Daddy gets a cookie, and you get one, too." As children grow older, they learn more sophisticated ways of sharing: offering their guests treats before taking one themselves, and taking turns.

Young children start out their social lives by playing alongside each other, engaging in what psychologists call "parallel play." That is, they enjoy each other's presence, and they notice each other, but they do not interact very much. At about age two and a half they can begin to actually play together. This represents an important step forward in a child's social development. It is at this point that he is ready to begin experimenting with the basics of sharing.

Two-and-a-half-year-old Thomas is playing with a set of wooden trucks when David, the same age, approaches and picks one of them up. Thomas immediately grabs it from him. Often at this point an adult will intervene, insisting that the child share, but it's usually better to allow the children to work it out themselves.

If Thomas refuses to share with David, he won't have a playmate for very long. And if he's left alone often enough, Thomas may begin to see that there are advantages to sharing, like having a playmate. In this instance, we might suggest to Thomas that perhaps David would like to join him in his play, but if he rejects the suggestion, we should not force the issue. We might tell David that perhaps Thomas would like to play with him a little later, and help him find another toy to play with. While we want our children to share with others, we also want to respect their right to create and maintain activities of their own choosing, and we want the decision to share, when it comes, to be theirs.

A child's natural curiosity often plays a role in this process. After being rebuffed by Thomas, David begins playing with a Noah's Ark set, a wooden boat complete with beautifully painted animals. Thomas glances over toward David. The animals are attractive, and it looks like David is having fun with them. Thomas continues to watch David with increasing interest. Finally he approaches David, holding a few of his trucks. He offers one of them to David to put on the ark. David responds by giving Thomas a pair of zebras to put in the trucks. The children are learning that playing together can be even more fun than playing alone.

As children grow older, we hope they will develop a spontaneous willingness to share with others. However, we cannot always count on their goodwill alone to carry the day. Sharing needs to make sense to a child and to not feel like a loss. We can often help arrange situations so that sharing is a winning choice.

Four-year-old Andy is visiting his best friend, Jeff, for an afternoon play date. In a room full of toys, Jeff sets up a clean piece of paper on an easel. Andy approaches him, saying, "I want to paint, too." Jeff responds by grabbing the paintbrush first. Seeing trouble brewing, Jeff's mom quickly brings over extra paintbrushes and a very large sheet of paper. "Here you go, guys," she says. "How would you like to make a painting together?" The boys are delighted now, for sharing means they both get more—bigger paper, more paint. Jeff's mom has made it easier for them to share.

Long before they have entered kindergarten, most children have mastered the basic concepts of sharing and ownership. Children of this age can understand the difference between owning, using, and borrowing possessions. They know what is theirs and what belongs to others, and they understand some things are for all to use. Whereas frantic cries of "Mine!" "No, mine!" "No, mine!" fill the air when toddlers are at play, one of the main things children are busy learning during the preschool years is how and when to share with others.

Of course, we have to understand that some possessions—a teddy bear, a special blanket—take on a deeply personal meaning to a child—they represent warmth, comfort, love, and security. When they're with their special thing, children feel a deep sense of belonging—the kind they feel when they're sitting in Mom's lap. Family members need to respect these objects. Children should not be asked to share their treasures. Nor should they be withheld as a disciplinary action or used to taunt a child. And if the precious item is threatened to be snatched away by a sibling or a visiting friend, the child should never be forced to relinquish it. We can explain to the taker that some things are not for sharing and that he or she must find something else to play with.

And remember, old "blankies" don't just fade away— they get washed up. (Some teddys, however, go to college— and beyond!)

"Take the Baby Back!"

One of the toughest things a young child can find herself having to share is her parents' attention upon the birth of a second child. It's natural for the firstborn to feel something's been taken from her. And the reality is, in some ways, it has. Her parents are now juggling the needs of two little people, a major leap in the demands on their time and energy. The birth of a third and any subsequent children is not as difficult as the arrival of the second, because by then the children are more used to sharing.

At first, four-year-old Daryl was excited to learn he was going to have a baby brother. He looked forward to being the "big guy" around the house. However, once the baby came home from the hospital, things weren't as much fun as he'd imagined.

"You never play with me anymore," he complained to his mother.

"You're right, Daryl," Mom sighed. She was bone tired. "Everything's different with the new baby. Maybe we could play Chutes and Ladders this afternoon while the little guy sleeps," she added, wishing she could take a nap then, too.

Daryl's parents had prepared him for the birth and were careful to express their appreciation to him for being a good big brother. They each tried to spend a little individual time with him every day. All the family and friends who visited were sensitive to Daryl's situation and paid extra attention to him: many even brought him gifts. All this helped ease the intensity of Daryl's feelings, but it didn't change the fact that he had lost his privileged position as the only child, and that he now had to share his parents with a very time-consuming infant. Adults know this is just a part of life, but to Daryl it is a serious injustice. We cannot return the new baby, as some new older siblings hopefully suggest, but we can give the child a fair hearing, take his feelings seriously, and do our best to give him his own special time.

Sharing Ourselves With Our Children

True generosity implies an openhearted willingness to give freely, without thought of personal gain or return. It means we give because someone has a need, and we care about them. Sacrifice or inconvenience may be involved, but we don't see it as a loss since this kind of sharing is inherently rewarding.

Surely, this describes a major aspect of what we do as

parents. We give to our children because they need us, and we give to them even more during some of their most difficult stages, putting our own needs aside to meet theirs. If we hope to be rewarded by them in some specific or immediate way, we are likely to be disappointed. What sustains us through the sacrifices we make for them is not the thought of return or reward, but the overwhelmingly strong feelings of love and concern we feel for them from the moment they are born.

The most important thing we can give our children is our presence and our attention. We must never forget that just being with our kids is nurturing to them at any age. However, sharing our time with them is sometimes the most difficult thing to do. Many parents are caught in a whirlwind balancing act of schedules. Between work, home, marriage, and the kids, many feel that "there just isn't enough of me to go around." The demands are even more intense for single parents.

One divorced father decided he wanted to spend some quality time with his eleven-year-old son. "Let's make a special plan to spend some time together, just you and me, okay?" His son's response was cautious. He eyed his father suspiciously and asked, quite seriously, "What would that be like?"

We cannot make up for lost time. It is far more important to use the time we do have together in meaningful ways. In this regard, we must be very honest with ourselves about the choices we make in our lives. When we tell ourselves, "I'll work hard now, putting in long hours, and after I've achieved a certain measure of success, I'll spend more time with my family," we may fool ourselves, but we won't fool our children. They will grow up with or without us, and then when we turn toward them, ready to spend more time with them, they may no longer be as receptive or available. We would be wiser to make it a priority to make time for our children all along. This is easier said than done. Financial and career pressures can make it very difficult to know when and where to draw the line. But it is important to try to always keep in mind how quickly our children will grow up, and try to be there, as much as we can be, for them.

Sometimes we may think we're spending time with our children, but in reality we are missing the connection. Frank's mother was an active volunteer for the youth group at church. When he was a member of the group, Frank was proud to have his mom be the one to chaperone their outings. However, as he grew older and became more active on weekend sports teams, a conflict of interests arose. Now his mom was frequently at youth group meetings, while he was out on the football field with no one to watch him from the stands. As the kind of person who was always willing to see a project through to its successful conclusion, Frank's mother found it difficult to give up her commitment to the group, even though it was now perhaps more important for her to be spending her time and energy elsewhere.

"Even Billy's mom is out there," Frank complained, "and he's on the bench most of the time."

Frank needs his mom's time and attention in a different way now. He wants her to be involved in what he is doing *now*.

Our time and energy are limited. We need to constantly reevaluate our priorities, our activities, and our commitments in light of our children's development. Sharing our time means we need to be flexible and to adjust as their needs evolve. We need to keep pace with the changes in their lives and to be there for them not only when they are small, but as they grow older, too.

Making the Most of Our Time Together

The way we spend time with our children is as important as the amount of time we spend. If we begrudge the time and energy we are giving, the message we send our children can be one of resentment or impatience rather than generosity.

Nine-year-old Julia has asked her mom to help her prepare a poetry reading for her school assembly. "Okay," Mom agrees briskly, "but let's make it quick. I have phone calls to return." Although Julia is glad to have her mom's help, she also feels rushed. Worse, she has a sinking feeling inside that her project is insignificant, just something to get through as quickly as possible, and that her mom's phone calls are more important.

When we give our time generously, our children know that the time we choose to spend with them is as at least as important as anything else in our lives. Though they need to learn that we cannot spend all our time attending to their needs, whether they are toddlers or teenagers, they should be able to have at least a few minutes of our undivided attention every day. It may be hard for us to find those few minutes some days, but it's not too much for them to ask.

Sharing With Those Who Have Less

Another level of sharing is reached when a child extends himself to help those who are in need. Often children are invited to participate in an organized effort through school or religious organizations—a food drive at Thanksgiving or a toy drive at Christmas. They are usually happy to participate in this type of sharing, for they recognize they have more than enough food and toys at home and it is not hard for them to understand how sad it is that someone might not have enough. They are not sacrificing anything, and they enjoy the feeling of goodwill that results when they join together with others in giving. We should be sure to take advantage of such opportunities for our children to learn the joy of sharing with those in need.

Once they become aware of the needs of others, some

children are moved to respond to those needs in a very direct way. We should encourage our children to act on their instincts to try to help others, even though doing so may lead to inconvenience or sacrifice on our part. They may need our help in coming up with ideas for things they could do to address the problems they see. A child might choose to give up some of his free time to do volunteer work, or contribute part of his weekly allowance to a worthy cause. Children can do amazing things on their own: One eleven-year-old boy started a blanket drive, which grew into a larger program that provided coats, hot coffee, and sandwiches to the homeless. Although adults helped him as his project grew, the boy remained central to the organization. He continued to work on the front line, delivering blankets and coats, and he appeared as the spokesperson to solicit donations.

The Fruits of Sharing

When children grow up in a family where sharing is a way of life, they experience the importance, as well as the joy, of giving. As they become teenagers, they begin to understand the kind of giving that parenting involves. At that point, they can begin to give back a bit.

Fifteen-year-old Sadie's mom stayed up late one night, helping her daughter study vocabulary words. In the morning she found a note from Sadie. "Thank you for staying up late with me. I really appreciate your help."

These are the moments that restore our faith in ourselves as parents. When our kids start complimenting us on what we've given them, we can rest assured they're on their way to knowing what generosity is all about. It's a big subject, and it takes a lifetime to learn it.

We hope our children will grow up knowing how to give of themselves without the thought of personal gain, to give as an expression of caring and belonging. We want them to share themselves, and to contribute to their community, giving their time, their energy, their attention, and their possessions. Not everyone achieves this level of generosity—but those who do live fulfilling lives, and they make the world a better place.

If children live with honesty, they learn truthfulness

Truthfulness is perhaps the most difficult thing of all to teach. For while most parents would agree that honesty and truthfulness are important qualities to develop in our children, the reality is that we are all, to some degree, less than completely honest in our day-to-day lives. And determining how, when, and to what degree honesty is important is a highly complex and very personal matter. Most of us tell our children stories we consider to be harmless, like the ones about Santa Claus and the Tooth Fairy, but some parents believe that even this kind of storytelling is a form of dishonesty. Some parents consider it acceptable to lie about their children's ages in order to get them free travel on an airplane or a reduced admission at the movies; others do not. No matter what our own personal standards, almost all of us at least occasionally tell "little white lies" designed to simplify our lives, to save time, or to spare others hurt feelings. However, when faced with similar dilemmas, we would not make the same decisions. There is no doubt about it, telling the truth can be a very murky business.

If it is not always easy for adults to know when telling the whole truth is the right thing to do and when it is better to shade the truth or even to lie, imagine how confusing it must be for our children. They know we value honesty and expect them to tell the truth, yet they witness our own inconsistency and discover that in certain circumstances, their truthfulness seems to distress us. How can we teach them the importance of being honest, while acknowledging how complicated it can sometimes be?

The Truth of the Matter

We can start by helping our children understand that honesty and truthfulness are different aspects of the same thing. Honesty covers a broad range of behaviors, including our ability to see and experience things as they are—without distortion, wishful thinking, avoidance, or denial. Truthfulness refers to our ability to communicate what we see and experience accurately and clearly. As they grow older, we also want to help our children develop a sense of discretion—the ability to discern situations in which it is better to leave the truth, or at least parts of it, unsaid. They likewise need to come to understand the difference between a lie and an honest mistake. Lying involves intentional deception, and it is the deception that is wrong, not just that a fact has been misstated.

The first step is to teach our children to recognize and face the truth, even when it is uncomfortable or undesirable for them to do so. We want them to be able to report to us fully and accurately what has happened in a given situation, or what they have done. This involves learning to distinguish between fact and various kinds of fiction—wishful thinking, reporting what we think others want to hear rather than what is so, or simply flights of imagination.

Children who have difficulty describing honestly how something happened are usually afraid of the consequences of being truthful, and are attempting to protect themselves or others from blame or punishment. We can help them by creating an environment in which they are praised for answering truthfully, even when they have done something wrong. There is a fine balance here. On the one hand, we need to help our children take responsibility for their wrong behavior and accept the consequenses. We don't want our children to think that no matter what they do, as long as they tell the truth everything is okay. On the other hand, we don't want them to be so fearful of our response to the truth, that they are tempted to lie.

One way we can help in this regard is by trying to focus on what happened instead of seeking to assign blame.

"How did a tennis racket get left out on the porch last night?" Mom asks her daughters, nine and eleven years old. The girls look at each other nervously, realizing they may be in trouble.

"Well," the younger daughter begins, "I carried it in from the car along with my backpack and the other stuff. I guess I dropped it on the porch so I could open the front door."

The older daughter chimes in, "I said I'd get it, but then I forgot to go back out to pick it up."

Mom gets the picture and makes a serious appeal to both daughters. "Please make sure it gets all the way inside next time. A racket can easily be ruined when it's left out all night."

Asking how the racket came to be on the porch gave Mom more accurate information about what happened than if she had asked who had left it there. If the focus were on who was responsible, the girls would have been inclined to blame each other. This way, they answered their mother truthfully, each reporting her own experience, and Mom held them both accountable for an understandable mistake.

Nothing but the Truth

Before they learn not to, all children experiment with lying. So one of the important skills we need to develop as parents is how to handle the situation when they do. It is a delicate matter. We need to confront them without frightening them, and we need to do so in such a way that they understand we are on their side. We should never try to deliberately trap them, or corner them into a situation where they are tempted to lie. But when we do catch them in a lie, we must be prepared to make a stand, and be sure they understand how important it is that they be truthful.

Four-year-old Erin and her mom have made cookies to take to the preschool bake sale. Later that afternoon, while Mom is working at her desk, Erin comes running in to tell her something. There are cookie crumbs and bits of chocolate on the outside of her mouth.

"Erin, I notice some chocolate crumbs on your face," Mom says. "Did you by any chance take a cookie from the baking rack?"

The little girl shakes her head. "No, Mommy," she answers wide-eyed.

Mom quickly realizes she is in a very delicate conversation. "Let's start over, honey," she says gently, "and please tell me the truth. Did you take one of the cookies we made? It's okay if you did, but I need to know."

"Well . . . maybe just a little one," Erin admits, licking her fingers.

"Just one?" asks Mom.

"No, two," says Erin.

"Now, is that the real truth?" Mom asks. Golden curls bob up and down proudly. "I'm glad you were honest, Erin," Mom says. "It's important to be truthful."

"Okay," says Erin. "But can I have another cookie?"

"Not now," Mom answers. "Number one, it's almost dinnertime, and number two, we need to save most of those cookies for your bake sale. That's why I'd like you to ask me first next time you want a cookie, so we can talk about it. Okay?"

"Okay, Mommy," Erin says. "Now can I go play?"

Mom has imparted an important lesson in this scenario, and helped Erin understand that it's important to be truthful with her mother even when she senses that perhaps her mother may be displeased with her action. She's also made it clear that getting at the truth is important enough to her that she will stop what she is doing, and talk with her daughter long enough to get at the truth of the matter. She has also explained the reasoning behind her not wanting Erin to eat the cookies, and why it's a good idea for Erin to ask permission in the future.

Since this infraction wasn't very serious, and Erin's mom was busy, she might have been tempted to let the matter go. But she would have missed a golden opportunity to let her daughter know that she values truthfulness. Other parents might have come down hard on Erin for lying or for taking the cookies, but in doing so, they might only be teaching her to become a better liar or more adept at sneaking treats. The principle of truthfulness between parent and child is of paramount importance, and it should be treated as such. But we want to do it in such a way that our children learn to be truthful because they respect our values and want to please us, not because they are afraid of us.

Stories vs. Lies

In teaching our children about the importance of truth, we run into another tricky problem—the difference between telling a story, and telling a lie. Children have wonderfully active imaginations, and we certainly don't want to discourage them from enjoying them. We want to be sure to leave room in our explanation of truthfulness for the pleasure that can be derived from the creation and telling of stories, and encourage them to share the fruits of their imagination with us as well as with others. If this matter is handled carefully, we can use our discussions about the nature of storytelling as one way of helping our children learn to distinguish between fact and fiction.

Two-year-old Anthony's mom is beside herself. She's late for an appointment, and she can't find her keys. "I don't get it!" she says. "I just had them. Where could they be?"

"I think the monster took them," says Anthony, gravely.

"Mmm, the monster," his mom repeats. "And do you happen to know where the monster put the keys?"

"In the toy box!" Anthony crows, cheerfully.

Mom reaches into the toy box and pulls out the keys. "Are you telling a story?" she says to Anthony. "I think you are! And I think the monster is really *you!*" Anthony giggles, as she reaches out and tickles him.

"Monster," she adds, mentally making a note to be sure to keep the car keys out of his reach, "the car keys are not to play with. If they get lost, we can't drive the car. Please don't take them again."

At this age, and in this situation, Mom has done all that is necessary in terms of clarifying the difference between truth and fiction, and she's done it in such a way that Anthony is able to understand that storytelling can be fun, especially when we all know it's "just a story."

We can create a home environment in which a distinction is drawn between the truth and storytelling, but stories are still enjoyed and appreciated. We can also help our children build an understanding about the nature of truth vs. fiction that will support them when they discover the reality behind treasured myths such as Santa Claus and the Tooth Fairy. Some parents may never find it necessary to say, "There is no Santa Claus." Instead, as their children become older and inevitably ask questions about the validity of the story, they can be guided toward a gradual awareness that Santa is a myth, while continuing to appreciate the mystery of belief that he represents.

Mom, Dad, and seven-year-old Kevin are driving in the car on their way to do some Christmas shopping. Suddenly, out of the backseat comes the question Kevin's parents have been dreading. "Is Santa Claus real?" Kevin asks.

"Paul's mom says Santa lives in the North Pole. Janie's father says Santa Claus is the spirit of giving. Mary's big sister says Santa is just an imaginary person. So, is he real or not?"

Mom takes a deep breath and carefully answers, "You know, Kevin, there are many, many things in the world we don't fully understand. Let's just let the Santa story be a wonderful mystery."

Kevin leans his head back against the seat and smiles. For now, this answer is enough to satisfy him. He wants to believe in Santa, and he's being allowed to. At the same time, his mother's answer is one that respects the growing maturity that has caused him to ask the question in the first place, and it leaves room for a changing understanding of who Santa Claus really is. As he grows older, he will be able to appreciate that his mother answered his question truthfully, though somewhat evasively, while gently guiding him toward developing a more mature perspective on the nature of Santa Claus.

Little White Lies

Some things are easy to characterize as true or false, and others are not. As children become involved in the world outside their home, they quickly encounter the reality that there are many points of view, and that in any given situation, each point of view is important to our total understanding of what is happening.

Seven-year-old Fran is upset with her mother, "You lied," she says. "On Sunday you said you loved Aunt Karen's dinner, but you just told Daddy her cooking was terrible."

"You're right," Mom agrees. "I didn't tell her what I really thought about her cooking because I didn't want to hurt her feelings. I thought it was more important to be kind than totally honest."

"Oh," Fran says. After thinking about that for a couple of minutes, she asks, "So, does this mean I don't have to be honest all the time?" She is trying hard to figure out what the rules are.

Mom gives her daughter her full attention. "I do want you to be honest," she says carefully. "But there are some situations in which it is more important to be kind. When we tell a little lie in order to keep someone's feelings from being hurt, it's called a 'white lie.' It is lying, but in some cases it's okay."

Fran is listening very attentively, but she is clearly confused.

"Look," Mom continues. "Suppose your friend Andrea came over to show you her new dress, and you didn't like it—you thought the color looked yucky. Would you tell her that?"

Fran thinks this over and says, "She wouldn't like that."

"Well, what could you say to her that would make her feel good?"

"Ummm . . . it's okay?" Fran looks less than satisfied with her own answer.

"Maybe," Mom says.

"I know, I could say something else I like about it!" Fran enthused.

"Yes, that's the idea," says Mom. "Find something nice you can say about it, or maybe ask her a question about where she got it or something. The important thing is that your friend is allowed to feel happy about something that's important to her. And you know," she adds, "it's important to remember that not everybody likes the same things. A color you're not crazy about might be her favorite color." Now Fran is learning not only about the importance of being kind, but is being reminded that there are many different ways of viewing the world, and that they all have validity.

Of course, this issue would not have come up at all if Mom had simply refrained from discussing her opinion of her sister's cooking in front of Fran. The old adage "If you can't say something nice, don't say anything at all," may have made some people overly reluctant to express their true feelings, but there is wisdom in it. Certainly, if we indulge in expressing all our feelings openly, even those that may upset our children, we should be prepared to take the time to discuss their concerns with them thoroughly, as Fran's mom did.

Teaching Our Children Integrity

Children learn what honesty is from their parents. What we do and what we say provide a living example of what it means to be honest. Our children notice how we handle the myriad situations life offers up, and when they are young, at least, they assume that our way is the right way to do things.

As nine-year-old Alicia and her father were leaving a restaurant after lunch, Dad absentmindedly stared at the change the cashier had given him. A few feet into the parking lot, he realized a mistake had been made in his favor.

"Just a sec, Alicia, something's wrong here." Dad said, holding out the change for her to see. "She gave me too much money back."

Father and daughter reviewed the arithmetic and discovered that they'd received about five dollars too much. "Let's go back in and straighten this out," Dad said.

Alicia wasn't quite as enthusiastic, since she was imagining how they could use the extra five dollars, but she knew her dad was right. The cashier was very grateful and explained that she would have had to make up the difference with her own money at the end of the day. The manager, overhearing their conversation, gave Dad a coupon for a big discount on their next visit. When father and daughter left the restaurant for the second time, they were both feeling pretty good.

"How about that, Alicia?" Dad said. "Are you glad we gave the money back?"

"I'd say honesty pays off," said Alicia.

"It feels good to do the right thing, even when you don't get a reward," Dad said. "But lots of times telling the truth makes nice things happen that we didn't expect."

Heart to Heart

There are times when total honesty is not appropriate. With some topics, it's more important that our answers take into consideration our children's age and level of maturity. Most of us err in the direction of underestimating our child's ability to understand, although there's always one parent in my family-living classes who goes into an overly detailed scientific explanation in response to their child's first inquiry about where babies come from, bewildering and overwhelming the child.

Sex and death are the most difficult issues to discuss with our children. Most of us are uncomfortable talking about these issues even with other adults. Explaining them to our children is very challenging. We have to gauge our child's ability to understand the concepts raised, and we have to consider how what we choose to tell them may affect them. Telling them too much about sex at too early an age may burden them with details they find perplexing or unsettling, and the concept of death can frighten them and interfere with their general sense of security.

We must remember that our children generally know, see, and hear far more about these topics than we imagine they do, although the information they glean and the assumptions they make may be highly inaccurate. When these subjects come up, one good way to begin the conversation is to ask our kids what they already know. That way we can start where they are and clear up any major misconceptions. Then we can share our most candid and age-appropriate explanations with them. Sometimes it is helpful to draw on outside resources to help in discussing these matters. There are many good picture books for young children and their parents, designed to help them discuss sex, death, and other difficult topics.

When we underestimate our children's understanding and try to cover the truth, our children notice the discrepancy between what they already understand and our explanations. This may confuse some children, and cause them to feel self-doubt or guilt. They are inclined to believe us, so when there is a discrepancy they may assume they must have been wrong, and that their thoughts are bad ones, asking themselves, "How could I have imagined such a thing? How terrible of me!" We don't want to put our children in the position of having to sort out the truth and find in the end that we are the ones who misinformed or misled them.

One of the major preoccupations of the teenage years is questing for the truth, along with the search for an identity independent of Mom, Dad, and family. The process of understanding their maturing bodies and forming a sense of individuality and uniqueness is just as challenging and just as powerful an experience as the efforts they made as tiny babies to reach out to grasp and hold on to objects in their crib. The teen is reaching out, too—trying to grasp the abstract, to master the ineffable meaning of self and other, to determine what his or her own principles for living will be, and attempting to anchor it all in the real world.

Their newly mature bodies also shape their thoughts and feelings. Unfortunately, when they don't feel comfortable asking us the questions that preoccupy them, they may ask other kids, and the kids they ask may be even more confused than they are. As a barrage of information comes at them, they try to sort it all out. During this difficult time, there is no more climbing on our lap to be comforted. However, this doesn't mean our children don't need us anymore. And no matter how distant they seem, or how brusquely they rebuff our attempts to be close to them, be assured they need us more than ever.

Our relationship is put to the test during these vital teen years. We must develop a new kind of closeness. Our adolescents want to feel close to us, and to know that we are with them. They need to know they can come to us anytime, to tell us how they feel, and that we will listen to their stories, will relate to their search for meaning, and will help them develop a broader view, a new view, or explore alternatives with them. They need to know that we will answer as fully and completely as we can their questions about sexuality, their developing bodies, their intense feelings and desires. How can we hold onto their trust in the middle of all this? By being honest and truthful with them.

As best you can, you need to set aside emotion, embarrassment, and any uncomfortableness you may feel. You need to communicate the information your kids will need to live and function in the world. Just as you prepared them for the first day of preschool, then kindergarten, then junior high, you need to prepare them to face adult issues. Today's world can be dangerous. Kids are exposed to drugs and alcohol in junior high or before, they are sexually active at a younger age, and they are vulnerable to a host of sexually transmitted diseases, with the threat of AIDS always looming large.

I suggest to the parents I work with that they set aside some time when they're not with the kids to talk about their own teen years, and try to remember what their parents told—or didn't tell—them. How honest and open were their parents? What did they need from them that they did not receive? What difference would this have made in their teen years? Could their parents have been more direct with them? How much information came from other kids? How much of it was accurate? Were they informed about the basics—menstruation, nocturnal emissions, erections, masturbation, orgasms, pregnancy, contraception—by their parents or by someone else? Most parents who do this exercise learn significant new things about each other and come up with some good stories to share with their teens.

If you don't know the answer to a question your child asks, just say so, and educate yourself by seeking out the best books, pamphlets, and articles you can find. It's your choice to move forward with all the honesty and truthfulness you can muster and give your teens the information they need. Of course, the most important thing you can give them is warmth and understanding, a close and caring relationship, and the knowledge that you are always there for them. Then you have to try to relax and hope they make good choices.

The Value of Truthfulness

R aising our children to be honest and truthful will help them in many ways. They will understand the value of integrity and trust in their personal relationships with colleagues, friends, and family. They will have the courage to look at themselves and their situations honestly, and to address truthfully their role and responsibility for taking constructive action. Perhaps most importantly, they will have the comforting knowledge that they are being honest with themselves. The peace of mind that comes from this knowledge is a great gift.

If children live with fairness, they learn justice

C hildren tend to be very practical about the idea of fairness. To them, fair means right and unfair means wrong. They are used to games with clear rules defining what's fair, and they expect everyone to abide by the same set of rules. Of course, this isn't what happens in real life—though we've all had moments when we wished there was a rule book for life that would tell us definitively the fair way to proceed, and that everyone would honor it.

As adults we're used to life's ups and downs, and the fact that things don't always turn out the way we think they should. For our children, the fact that life isn't always fair hasn't settled in yet. They keep thinking it should be, and are frustrated when it's not. When seven-year-old Sally mournfully complains to her mother that the neighborhood game of kick the can wasn't fair, her mother may be tempted answer glibly, "Life's not fair." But this kind of response doesn't address Sally's legitimate concerns. She needs to discuss how she feels the game wasn't fair, how she hoped it would turn out, and what she expected. If Mom explores these questions with Sally and listens attentively and patiently to her complaints, she can gradually work the conversation around to be more positive, by asking, "How do you think it should have been?" and "What could be done to make it work better next time?" Focusing on what can be done differently in the future may help Sally balance her feelings of disappointment with optimism that her next experience playing the game will be a better one.

Such discussions can also help to ease the tension when there is disagreement within the family about what's fair. An open dialogue allows family members to share their unique viewpoints and explain how they might do or see things differently next time. Unfortunately, no matter how conscientiously we strive to be fair, we cannot always satisfy everybody.

As parents, we may like to think our idea of fairness is just, but we need to remember that each family member will see things differently, and that justice is often defined by who is doing the viewing. What's important is that our children understand that our *intention* is to be fair, and that they know we are open to discussing their ideas and concerns. Taking the time to hear our kids out, helping them sort through their feelings, and encouraging them to put their best ideas into practice is one way to show that we care about fairness in everyday life.

Fairness in the Family

Whenever I hear a parent claim, "I treat all my kids the same," I know it can't be true. This is just not humanly possible. And even if it were, it's not necessarily desirable. Our children need our attention to be directed specifically toward their own unique strengths and weaknesses. What might be fair for one child in a family could be unfair to the next. Different ages, different needs, different situations, and different personalities all call for different approaches.

Despite our best efforts to treat our children fairly, sibling rivalry is alive and well in most families. The fights may seemingly be about toys, special privileges, food, or money, but often the underlying problem is perceived favoritism. Children can be very sensitive to the ways parents express and distribute their energy, time, interest, and attention. The bottom line is that each child wants to feel as important, and as loved, as the others.

When kids complain of favoritism, it might be worth taking a moment to examine our true feelings and the attitudes we may be conveying. It's inevitable that competition will arise and that siblings will be compared to each other. But we should make sure that we are not unintentionally fostering an atmosphere of rivalry in the home. Sometimes seemingly innocuous strategies for getting things done may have side effects we hadn't thought about. For example, encouraging kids to compete against each other to finish chores or get their homework done first might be a setup for strife. Winning, losing, who's first, who's last—these concepts belong on the athletic field, not in the home. We want brothers and sisters to evaluate their own behavior and skills, to compare themselves to themselves, not to each other.

One way to counteract feelings of favoritism is to spend special time with each of your children individually. One set of parents I know has three sons, ages four, six, and eight. Each parent takes a turn inviting one boy out for a simple meal, like a pancake breakfast at a coffee shop. This gives them a time to be together and talk without the usual distractions and competition inherent in the home setting. The parent learns what's on the child's mind— what's happening at school, in the neighborhood, at home with his brothers—and the child gets to have one of his parents all to himself for a little while. Such conversations, away from the bustle and confusion of the household, are especially important because they lay the groundwork for open communication during the tough teenage years. They also very clearly send an important message to each child: "You are important to us, and we care about how you're feeling." The meals don't have to take place in a restaurant, but it helps if they are away from the home. In fact, they don't have to be meals at all: a special outing that affords a chance to talk—a hike, a visit to a museum, a boat ride—can work equally well. The most important thing is that the child feels he is getting your undivided attention—some special time for himself.

Speaking Up

In order for our children to learn the lesson that they can speak up in the face of what they consider to be unjust—whether it be at school, in the neighborhood, or, later, in the workplace—they need to practice expressing their feelings with us first. If we respect their protests about what they see as unfair in the family, they will learn that they can help change things for the better.

"You treat me like a baby," nine-year-old Andy complains to his parents after dinner one evening. "My friends get to stay up as late as they want."

"As late as they want?" his father asks, looking over his reading glasses.

"Later than I do, anyway," Andy says.

"Who do I have to tickle awake every school morning?" his mom asks.

"Me," admits Andy.

"It seems like you need the sleep you get," Dad says.

"What about on weekends?" Andy asks.

"Well, weekends are a little different. We can talk about a new weekend bedtime, if you like," Mom says. "How late do you think you should be able to stay up on Fridays and Saturdays?" By using the word "should," she's encouraging Andy to use his best judgment, not just tell her what he wants. This elevates the negotiation, and helps Andy to be responsible in deciding what kind of changes he'd like to see.

"I guess I still need at least eight hours sleep, so that means . . ." Andy says, as he figures out his new bedtime.

"Okay," Dad says. "Let's try it."

"Great!" Andy says. He's pleased with himself for having changed a situation he thought was unfair.

When our children think a family rule is unfair, it's very important that they be allowed, even encouraged, to question it. If we do not take their feelings seriously, and respect their right to express themselves openly, our children may fall into a pattern of resentful acquiescence. This damages our relationship and drives a wedge between us. It's better to be somewhat flexible about family rules and encourage our children to assert themselves when they think they are faced with an injustice. This helps them maintain a positive attitude toward working problems out within the family and gives them the mind-set to advocate for justice as they enter other situations in their lives.

Betsy came home from fourth grade one day with tears in her eyes. "My teacher never calls on me," she complained. "I know the answers and I raise my hand, but she just ignores me."

Betsy's mom listens with concern. "Who does the teacher call on?" she asks.

"She lets the boys talk and they never know the right answer," Betsy says sulkily.

"Does she call on the other girls?" Mom asks.

"Not much," Betsy pauses, then brightens. "It's not just me. She ignores all the girls."

"That doesn't sound fair," Mom answers. "What do you think we can do about that?"

"You could write her a letter," Betsy suggests.

"I could," Mom says, adding "Any other ideas?"

"You could come in and talk to her," Betsy says.

"I like that idea," Mom says, "And then the three of us could talk together. How does that sound?"

Mom is not only acting as an advocate for her daughter, she is showing her that she, too, can take action to change a situation that isn't right. With her mom's support, Betsy is learning how to assert herself so that her voice is heard.

Taking Action

It's inevitable that our children will witness and experience injustice in their lives. In some of these situations they will be the victims—of a coach or teacher who plays favorites, or of other children who are behaving cruelly. Other situations will challenge them to stand up for someone else's rights when they are being treated badly. If they have had some practice, and some success in combatting injustice in their own home, they will be more likely to be able to speak up for themselves and others when they encounter problems outside the home.

While walking to school, ten-year-old Michael notices some boys he knows from his class surrounding another kid in the corner of the school parking lot. When he gets closer he sees that the kid is being picked on, possibly because he's from a different cultural background.

Michael is nervous and not sure what to do. Without really thinking, he walks over to the group and calls out to the boy who's being picked on, "Come on, Tom, it's almost time for class." All the kids turn and look at him, surprised, and Tom, sensing an opening, follows Michael toward school.

It took courage for Michael to do what he did. It always takes courage for an individual to confront a group, even in the low-key way that Michael chose. It would have been much easier for him to pretend he didn't see anything or hope that a teacher would intervene. His parents may never hear about the incident or their son's involvement. Many kids don't tell their parents everything about their experiences outside the home. If Michael's parents knew, they would be proud of having raised a child who has a strong sense of justice, who believes that everyone has the right to be treated fairly, and who is willing to risk his own comfort in order to help someone in trouble.

Sometimes kids are confronted with injustice on a bigger scale than they can address on their own. Thirteen-year-old Stella was watching a news magazine television show with her parents one evening. One of the show's segments was about migrant fruit-pickers' living conditions, and how difficult it was for them to earn enough to start a new life. Stella was deeply upset by what she learned. She turned to her parents and said, "That's not fair. How can they live like that? The farmers should build better places for them to live and pay them more. I make more an hour when I help Mrs. Simmons watch her kids."

Her parents weren't quite sure what to say. After a minute, Stella's mom said, "It is a terrible situation, honey, and I think it's great that you're concerned. One of the sad facts of life is that there is a lot of injustice in this world."

"But can't somebody do something about it?" Stella persists. "Can't the government tell those farmers to treat their workers more fairly or something?"

"That's an interesting idea, and maybe there is a legislative solution down the road. But in the meantime, do you think there's anything we could do to help the situation now?" Mom asked.

"I don't know. They're so far away. Send them some money or something?" Stella suggested tentatively.

"Maybe there's an organization that helps them," Dad piped up. "You know how there's a homeless shelter for the homeless and a soup kitchen for the hungry here? And how the Red Cross helps people in need? Maybe there's a group that helps migrant workers. We could check the show's Web site and see if they offer any information."

"Good thinking," Mom said. "If there were such a group and it seemed like they were doing good work, would you be interested in giving them some money, Stella?"

"You mean *my* money?" Stella asked.

"Well, yes," Mom said. "And if you give, I'll match your contribution. Better yet, I'll double it." Stella looked pensive.

"Sweetie," Dad said gently, "trying to help right the wrongs in this world usually involves some sacrifice."

With a little lingering reluctance, Stella said, "I guess I could send a week's allowance."

"Okay, let's go on-line and see what we can find," Dad said, getting up.

"I'm proud of you for wanting to help, Stella," Mom added, giving her shoulder a squeeze.

With her parents' help, Stella is empowered to take steps to help right an unjust situation, albeit in her own small way. Instead of feeling helpless in the face of a societal problem, she is trying to make a difference.

Justice as an Ideal

Justice is a big subject, one of the biggest. But our children's sense of fairness starts with small things. If we treat their concerns about being treated fairly with respect, they will have the foundation they need to extend the same kind of respect to others. It's a big leap from the subject of their rights within the home to the rights of people around the world, but with our help, they can see that the building of a world "with justice for all" is something we can work on together, and that doing so is one of the most important human challenges.

If children live with kindness and considera-tion, they learn respect

C hildren cannot be taught to be respectful. They can be taught to be polite, and to give the appearance of being respectful, but this is not the same as feeling genuine respect, and the two should not be confused. Children learn respect when they observe their parents treating each other and the members of their own family in a kind, considerate, respectful way, and they grow up thinking that the way they have been treated is the way to treat others.

Kindness and consideration are the hallmarks of re-spect: they can be expressed in thousands of small ways, day by day, week by week, year by year. Our willingness to extend ourselves for each other as well as for our children teaches them how to respect others. Through our example, we can show our kids that respect includes accepting other people as they are, acknowledging that their needs are as important as our own, and that sometimes the needs of others must even come first. As our children begin to show respect for others in small ways—when they are gentle with animals, or patient with younger siblings—we should be sure to praise them for their consideration, reinforcing the behavior and encouraging them to continue to grow in this direction.

The qualities of kindness and consideration take a long time to mature in all of us. As parents, we must admit that there are times when we fail to behave in ways that are respectful of each other or of our children. Admitting our shortcomings, apologizing for any hurt feelings we may have caused, and trying to be more mindful in the future helps heal whatever damage we may have done, and keeps us moving toward a better tomorrow. This openness will also show our children that learning how to respect others is a never-ending process, a learning adults are involved in as well as children.

Thinking of Others

It's only natural for very young children to be primarily concerned with themselves. Babies and toddlers think the world revolves around them and that other people exist to meet their needs. This self-centered orientation is natural at their stage of development. The understanding that others have needs as important as their own dawns slowly and gradually as children mature. The ability to find a balance—to consider others' needs while pursuing their own—takes even longer.

Our finest moments of parental guidance may occur in small, spontaneous situations that present us with the opportunity to teach our children how to be kind. We need to be alert to these moments, and use them to guide our children toward behavior that is considerate of others.

I recently noticed a mother in the grocery store with her two sons, aged approximately four and eight. They were stocking up on cat food when an elderly shopper dropped her purse, and the contents scattered on the floor. The older son immediately stopped what he was doing to help the woman retrieve her belongings. The younger boy kept piling cat food into the cart, until his mother subtly redirected him, suggesting to him without using words, that he might help his brother. First she softly touched his arm to get his attention, and to get him to stop what he was doing. Then she nodded her head in the direction of the scene unfolding before them. When the younger boy saw what his older brother was doing, he joined in to help. In her gentle way, this boy's mother gave him a powerful lesson in treating others kindly.

Another way we can teach our children how to show kindness and consideration is through imaginary play. As four-year-old Kenny and his mom are straightening up his room before bed one night, Mom takes a moment to tuck Teddy Bear into bed with a gentle pat.

"There. I'll bet Teddy is comfy now," she says, with satisfaction.

Kenny moves over to the bear and rearranges the blankets, saying, "Sleep tight, Teddy."

Mom knows that Kenny has strong feelings of attachment toward Teddy, and she may have unconsiously decided to model kindness and considerate behavior toward "another" that he could easily relate to. Kenny enjoys the fact that his mom is entering his world of play, and is showing interest in something he loves. He also learns a lesson about how to show tenderness and concern toward something that needs nurturing.

We can also help our children develop a deeper sense of respect and empathy by asking them to imagine how another child may be feeling in a certain situation.

Jenny and Maria, both seven years old, are in the middle of a board game when a disagreement arises over the rules. Maria leaves abruptly and goes home. Jenny wanders into the kitchen to talk with her mom. "Maria's such a bad sport," she says. "She was losing, so she quit."

"What happened?" her mother asks. "Maria usually loves to play games."

Jenny explains the disagreement, blaming Maria.

"I'm sorry the game ended like that," Mom says thoughtfully. "I wonder how Maria's feeling."

"Huh? I don't know," Jenny answers as if surprised by the thought. She thinks it over for a minute, then says, "Maybe I'll call her."

When the girls talk, they manage to see that each of them was partly right, and partly wrong. Talking about it clears the air, and they're ready to play together again the next day. Hopefully they are also better prepared to communicate more effectively the next time there is a misunderstanding.

Mom's well-timed and sensitive questions have helped Jenny move beyond her own self-interest to consider Maria's point of view. Mom's concern for Jenny's friend encourages Jenny to take an active interest in how her friend might be feeling after a disagreement, an important element in creating a long-term friendship.

These lessons aren't self-evident, and they aren't that easy to put into practice, so our children need our help. If they don't master the essential skills for maintaining relationships while they are growing up, life will be far more difficult for them than it has to be.

Communicating Respect

Another way we express our respect for others is by being helpful and considerate in our communication with each other—what we say as well as the way we say it. "See your brother's paint box over there? Yeah, the one that's open. Close it, would you? Thanks," conveys a very different message than, "Your brother's paint box is open. Let's close it so his paints won't dry out. He'd be so disappointed if they were ruined." In the second case, the child is being given a much richer, fuller message that teaches the importance not only of respecting the materials we work with, but of looking out for and helping each other.

We can let our children know what we expect of them in a way that is respectful of them and their feelings. If Dad has to work one night, for example, it's wise to let the kids know ahead of time that he will need everybody to choose quiet activities for the evening because he has to concentrate. Telling them in advance gives the kids the opportunity to help their father by being considerate of his needs. It's also far more effective than yelling at them to quiet down, with little or no warning or explanation.

We can also encourage expressions of kindness and consideration in our children by noticing and acknowledging their caring behavior. Five-year-old Matthew helps his baby sister by picking up a toy she has dropped from her high chair and handing it back to her. "Thank you, Matthew," Dad says. "It's really nice that you're helping your baby sister out." Dad's noticing and appreciating Matthew's kindness is important: it gives Matthew the model he needs to follow and it rewards him for being kind.

Respecting Each Other

Everyone in the family is entitled to respect for his or her own possessions, as well as to a measure of privacy. The way we treat our possessions can generate a caring or uncaring attitude in little ones. Children notice our attitude toward our own belongings—when clothes are piled on the floor, tools left out in the yard, doors slammed, they see it all, and they walk in our footsteps.

It isn't only our treasured items that deserve our respect. Everyday household items do, too. No matter how modest the home, or how big the family, every child needs the right to have some personal possessions, things that no one else will use without asking permission.

It's also important to grant our children privacy. When they are very young, they need a great deal of help with dressing, bathroom activities, and grooming. As they grow older, they gradually take over these tasks for themselves, and as they do, they develop a sense of modesty about their bodies and a greater need for privacy. Children should be taught that they have a right to this privacy, as well as how to ask for it when they need it. They should also be taught to respect the privacy of others: to knock on doors that are closed and wait for permission to enter, for example. This makes it possible for Mom and Dad to retain some privacy, too.

Preadolescent girls especially need our support and understanding when they begin to mature. When their bodies begin to grow and change, they may need extra privacy, and it's important for everyone in the family to respect that. If a brother or sister, or even an aunt or uncle, is snickering or giggling over a child's budding modesty, we should remind them that to the child undergoing the changes, it's anything but a laughing matter, and they need our support and understanding, not our teasing.

Doing as We Do, Not as We Say

Possibly the most influential relationship our children observe is the one between their parents. This is where they are most likely to learn how respect is expressed in daily living. No matter what we tell our children about how to behave, the way we act toward each other is the message they will actually receive.

It's been a day full of bickering between the eight-year-old twins, Anna and Emily. Mom finally loses her patience and yells, "Stop fighting, I can't stand it anymore!"

Both girls look up at her in surprise and then Anna replies, "But you and Daddy argue all the time. This isn't any different."

Mom is speechless. She's never thought of it this way before, but she knows Anna is right.

Our children notice the way we speak to each other: our tone of voice, our attitudes, our unexpressed emotions. It's not simply a matter of whether we fight or argue. It's the way we resolve disagreements, how we communicate with each other in clearing up minor misunderstandings, and how well we respond to each other's needs.

Even the smallest gestures of attentiveness and concern that pass between Mom and Dad are noticed by our children, becoming a mental model for how to treat loved ones. When they hear the expressions of polite interaction—"please," "thank you," and "you're welcome,"—

used in a habitual and natural way, and when thoughtful questions such as "Can I get you something?" and "Can I help you with that?" are in the background of their everyday lives, they see the way people can help each other through life in both big moments and small.

Respecting Each Other's Differences

Our children will grow up to share their world with people of different beliefs, colors, and customs. An atmosphere of kindness, consideration, and tolerance for individual differences within the family will prepare them to respect the rights and needs of others. As they mature, we hope they will recognize the humanity within every person they meet. No matter what our differences, as humans we all share the same essential dreams and desires. We hope our children will discover we are more alike than different in our physical, emotional, and spiritual needs.

As they move into the larger world, and honor others out of a basic respect for individual worth and dignity, they can expect to be so honored in return. Growing up in an atmosphere in which kindly actions and active concern are a part of everyday life paves the way for them to practice respect and tolerance of others in their lives. Down through the ages, the great teachers of all the world's religions have agreed that it is through small, everyday acts of kindness that we make our mark in the school of life.

If children live with security, they learn to have faith in themselves and in those about them

We are the first custodians of our children's trust. They need to know that we will be there for them, no matter what: this is what it means to feel secure. When they know they can count on us to respond to their needs, consider their feelings, and respect them, they learn to trust us. And it is out of this security and our unwavering support that they develop faith in themselves.

I recently attended a piano recital where I witnessed a ten-year-old boy valiantly struggle through one of the pieces from *The Nutcracker*. He hadn't practiced quite enough, and by the end it was clear that he realized this. The audience gave him an encouraging round of applause anyway. After leaving the stage, the boy went straight to his mother and climbed into her lap. She held him comfortably through the next few pieces.

Now, this child was rather large to be sitting in his mother's lap, and I happen to know that the mother is very strict about her children keeping up with their piano practice. But at that moment, none of that mattered to her. Her message to her son was pure and simple: I am here for you, even when you stumble, and I am not afraid or embarrassed to show it.

Our children need to know that we will always stand behind them, and that our support is not dependent upon how well they complete the tasks before them, or how clumsily they may fall short at times.

Living With Faith

Faith is a word that is often used in a religious or spiritual context to describe a belief in God, or trust in the universe we live in. There are many ways to approach the concept of faith. Many people who do not regard themselves as religious understand the meaning of faith in their own way, and take comfort in some form of spirituality. Certainly it has been well established that people who have faith in something larger than themselves tend to deal with life's stresses better than those who don't. Let us define faith very broadly, thinking of it as confidence in one's own beliefs and values and in the world at large. This basic faith in the goodness of humankind is critically important in order to be able to face life with optimism and to trust others.

A Safety Net

Children develop faith in themselves gradually, over the years. From the time a young child says, "Me. I do it myself!" we know she is building confidence in herself. Our job is to give our kids the chance to test their skills and abilities while supporting them as they learn, reach out for new experiences, and make their forays into the unusual. There is a delicate balance to be achieved here. For our children to grow up feeling secure, we must give them enough time and space to experiment, to learn for themselves, or even fail, all the while remaining available to encourage, guide, and help them along the way.

Five-year-old Nicholas is neatly tucked into bed one night when he tells his mom, "I want the training wheels off my bike, okay?"

"Sure," Mom says, and the next morning they get out the screwdriver and remove the training wheels. But riding it isn't so easy and Nicholas is pretty shaky, especially when Mom takes her hand off the seat of the bike and he's on his own.

That night Nicholas says, "Could you put my training wheels back on?"

"Sure," Mom says. "We'll do that in the morning."

The next morning, Nicholas faces his "big-boy" bike again.

"Do you want to try it one more time before I put the training wheels back on?" Mom asks in an offhand way, knowing the next time might be the charm.

"Okay," Nicholas agrees. He's fairly relaxed, because

his mom's casual manner makes him feel he's got nothing to lose in giving it another try.

And that's it: Nicholas takes off, holding tightly to the handlebars, a big grin on his face, his faith in himself soaring. Mom has found just the right balance: she accepted Nicholas's request to return to the training wheels, yet also challenged him to try again. She didn't pressure him to be a "big boy" when he wasn't ready, and she made it easy for him to try "just one more time."

Will Nicholas fall? Yes, of course he will. We all fall sometimes, especially when we have the courage to push our limits. But that's when we need faith in ourselves the most, in order to get back on the bike.

Predictable, Dependable, Consistent

Our children rely on us to do what we say we will do, when we promised we would do it, and if we can't, to let them know. They believe what we tell them, and trust that we will follow through. And if we come through for them most of the time, they learn to depend on us.

We make countless promises to our children during their growing-up years. *We* may not think of them as promises, but *they* do. If we say we will pick them up at a certain time, they expect us to do so. If we are chronically late or forgetful, our children will learn that they can't trust us, and they will rightfully feel neglected.

When we can't show up on time because of a last-minute emergency, we should call and let our children know. We should show them the same consideration we would show a client or our supervisors at work. Children who are left waiting, who are always the last ones to be picked up, get a very sad look on their faces. You can see them trying to hide their disappointment and concern, but they're not very good at it.

Swimming class at the Y is over, and Mom shows up late again. Seven-year-old Mandy heaves a sigh of relief as she climbs into the car. Mom starts apologizing, explaining why she is once again the last parent to arrive. Mandy doesn't say much, just stares into space. She has given up on her mother. It's more important to her now to lower her expectations, and try to protect herself from feelings of disappointment and insecurity, than to give her mother another chance. Her mom is just not reliable, and Mandy knows it. She has adapted to the situation, but at what a price: this pattern of lateness has damaged both her opinion of her mother and of herself. After all, Mandy concludes, if she were really important to her mother, wouldn't her mom see how hard it is for her to always be the last one waiting, and try to do something about it?

I recently overheard some fourth-grade girls planning to go to a Saturday afternoon movie together. One girl said to another, "Let's get your mother to drive. Then we're sure to get there on time." All the other girls nodded their heads in assent. They knew exactly which mother was most dependable.

Dependable Doesn't Mean Boring

It's important to provide a secure environment for our children. There are so many unknowns in their lives, so much that's new and that they are learning, that a predictable, comfortable home helps give them a comforting measure of control. Nonetheless, we can still leave room for spontaneous, fun times.

Elaine's aunt comes over for dinner one Saturday night. At about eight o'clock, she looks around the living room and asks, "Anyone up for a movie?"

Mom and Dad are settled into the sofa. Eleven-year-old Elaine perks up, "Yeah, me!" she says, enthusiastically.

"Isn't it too late?" Mom asks. "The movies start around seven."

Elaine looks at her mom with pleading eyes. "Not really," the aunt replies. "Elaine and I can catch the late show. If we leave now, we can walk around the mall, maybe get some ice cream, first."

"The late show?" Dad says. He's about to protest, but he decides against it. Elaine will be up way past her usual bedtime, but it's not a school night, and this spontaneous outing is an excellent way for Elaine to get to know her aunt better. He turns to Mom and says, "Why not? She can sleep in tomorrow, and this will give Elaine and Susan some time together."

"Fair enough," Mom agrees. "Just come home right after the movie," she says. "And have a good time."

Routines are good and important for helping our children develop the security that comes from having a predictable schedule. But the times we allow them to depart from the routine are important, too. These are often the moments children remember all their lives. They're out of the ordinary, exciting, and new.

Elaine gets home around midnight. She has enjoyed the movie, the time with her aunt, even the night air. "You know it even smells different at night," she says. "Fresher!" She hugs her parents good-night and thanks them for letting her go.

Confidence Is Believing in Yourself

Our children need faith in themselves and how they see things in order to take action. If they don't trust their own decisions or have confidence in themselves, it's very difficult for them to be self-assertive. One of the ways we can help them develop this faith is to have faith in them ourselves.

Ten-year-old Andrew calls home from camp with a story about one of his cabin mates. "He asked me to be his canoeing partner, but when I got down to the lake, he'd buddied up with someone else," Andrew complains.

"Then he borrowed my army knife and didn't return it. And he told me I look like a duck when I run."

Dad is listening intently to his son 150 miles away. He wants to get in the car, drive up there, and talk with the camp director. Instead, he takes a deep breath and asks his son, "How are you going to handle this?"

Andrew answers, "Well, I went canoeing with another guy. And if I look like a duck, it's a pretty fast one, 'cause I came in third in the race."

"Way to go," Dad says.

"And I'm just going to tell him I want my knife back," Andrew continues. "I need it for the big hike. If that doesn't work, I'll talk to my counselor."

"You'll get it," Dad reassures him.

Andrew had confidence in his decision that his cabin mate's behavior was unacceptable as well as faith in himself to handle the situation. I know this sounds obvious, but there are children who would choose to ignore the problem because they lack the inner security to tackle it. Andrew's dad showed his confidence in his son by believing in his ability to handle the situation on his own.

We want our children to have a basic trust in themselves and in others. We hope they will have positive expectations of other people, yet recognize when the behavior of others is unacceptable. We also hope they will be dependable in their relationships and live up to their promises.

Faith in the Future

We will not be present for our children throughout their lives. However, if we can empower them with a solid sense of security during their childhood, the benefits will stay with them into adulthood. By helping them learn to believe in themselves, we will give them the confidence they need to be secure with others and to be good parents to their children, our grandchildren.

This is a gift to their futures. Our children's belief in themselves will guide their career choices, enabling them to take risks, handle responsibility, and trust their decisions. Their faith in others will enable them to fall in love, make meaningful commitments to others, and build families.

Without inner confidence and belief in themselves, our children will have a hard time enjoying life even when things go well, and a very difficult time when they encounter life's challenges. If they do have confidence in themselves—in their basic competence, goodwill, and overall abilities—there is little they cannot achieve if they set their minds to it.

We can help provide our kids with a sense of basic worth or worthlessness. It's a heavy responsibility, but it's actually very easy to fulfill. All we have to do is believe in them and in their good intentions. Then we have to let them know, beyond the shadow of a doubt, that this is the way we feel. They'll do the rest.

If children live with friendliness, they learn the world is a nice place in which to live

Our children's first world is the family. From us they learn what to value, how to behave, and what to expect from life, through thousands of seemingly insignificant moments in the course of day-to-day family living. Often our children pick up some of the strongest messages about our values and our behavior when we are least aware they are paying attention.

How friendly is this first world we give our children? Do we speak to them politely, with common courtesy? Do we accept them as they are rather than try to make them be who we want them to be? Do we give them the benefit of the doubt, trusting that their intentions are usually good ones? Are we curious about and eager to share their newest interests?

A friendly home environment is one in which children's efforts are encouraged, recognized and praised; where their mistakes, shortcomings, and individual differences are tolerated; where they are treated fairly and with patience, understanding, kindness, and consideration.

Certainly there are times when we have to exert parental authority over our children, but we can do so in a way that is friendly and warm, yet firm, rather than controlling or cold. We can create a supportive family environment and have positive expectations of our children, and still set boundaries for them.

Everyday family life creates the patterns our children will recreate in their homes when they are grown. We want to develop relationships with our children that are healthy, resilient enough to withstand the inevitable moments of family friction, and sturdy enough to survive into their adulthood. We want them to enjoy getting together for holidays and family celebrations, especially after they start families of their own. We want them to grow up with a positive outlook that will help them find their place in the world and enjoy what the world has to offer.

The Woven Web

We often take for granted the countless interactions we have with each other in daily family life. These interactions can serve as the basis for a well-developed ability to get along with others. Just as we are the models for our children, the family is the model for a social unit. In many ways, the situations our children will encounter in the neighborhood, at school, in the workplace, and in their communities will be similar to those they encounter in the family. In negotiating over and learning to share the bathroom, the computer, the TV, or the family car, we come to understand the meaning of responsibility and how we really do rely on each other.

Consider, for example, the cleanup after Thanksgiving dinner. It was nine-year-old Joey's job to empty the dishwasher after breakfast, but in all the excitement, he forgot. This makes the whole process of cleaning up more difficult. Eleven-year-old Kristin has been clearing the table, but there's nowhere to put the dirty dishes, which are now stacked on every countertop in the kitchen. Mom is trying to put the leftover turkey in the fridge, but has nowhere to work. Aunt Lucy is at the kitchen sink, starting to wash the pots. Meanwhile, the food is hardening on the dinner plates, and there are too many people in the kitchen. Dad brings out the after-dinner coffee and needs a dozen cups to go around, but most of them are still in the dishwasher. All in all, a typical slice-of-life in the chaotic world of the family.

Mom quickly realizes the source of the problem and calls into the dining room, "Joey, we need you to come empty the dishwasher. We've got big trouble in here."

Joey jumps up from the table, realizing he's forgotten his chore on the worst possible day. He quickly empties the dishwasher with a little help from his sister, and the gridlock in the kitchen is soon resolved.

Through this incident, Joey can easily see how his behavior affects the rest of the family. Although this example may be exceptionally clear-cut, our interdependency is just as much a factor in everyday family living. In fact, learning how to cooperate with each other in a friendly manner will teach our children valuable lessons about how to get along with others in the larger world. The better they are at contributing their efforts to a common goal, and pulling together to work as a team, the better they will be liked by their friends, neighbors, and coworkers, and the more welcoming the world will seem to them. And if they learn to contribute to whatever worlds they are entering with grace and generosity, they will in fact be instrumental in making the world a nicer place to live.

"It Takes a Village"

The structure of the family is changing. Fewer children are growing up with both Mom and Dad. Many are being raised by single parents, grandmothers, or other relatives, while others have two moms or two dads. No matter what the makeup of the family is, the most important thing for our children is to know that they are wanted and loved.

The more friendly, caring adults there are in our children's lives, the better off they will be. Our children benefit from regular, casual contact with extended family—which may include close family friends. Since we can't be everything at all times to our children, there are times when it is beneficial for everyone to have friends and family step in, adding a fresh perspective, a little extra time, or their own special talents.

Nine-year-old Jimmy is frustrated with his model airplane project. He needs adult help and support, but Dad is too busy, and frankly, he just doesn't have the patience. Grandpa, on the other hand, is happy to spend the time with Jimmy and loves every minute of helping him glue parts together.

It's this kind of quality time together that allows children to feel surrounded by the love and wisdom of an older generation. Often, grandparents have more time to give their grandchildren than they had for their own children. They may not be as busy as they were then, and their priorities in life also may have shifted, from work to family. I teach a special Family Living class for grandparents, and I find that grandmothers often need to talk about what they felt they missed doing when they were raising their own families. One regret expressed over and over is, "I should have played more with my children and not been so busy." They realize that taking the time to play with their children, and develop friendships with them, is a rich and healing activity that can benefit the whole family.

The extended family can also serve as a safety net for our children. The more people involved, the closer the weave of the net, the better able we are to catch and support our children in times of need.

Megan's Aunt Dale would often surprise her twelve-year-old niece by picking her up at school. Dale would take Megan out for ice cream or hot chocolate, and sometimes she'd take Megan and her girlfriends to the local swim club. Once she took them all to the city to see a musical. When Megan ran into some trouble with kids at school and was hesitant to talk to her parents about it, she turned to Dale. Dale was available and ready to listen. Most important, she loved Megan and Megan considered her "family." It can be a relief to parents lucky enough to have a close, extended family to know that when their children are, for whatever reasons, reluctant to turn to them to discuss their problems, there is someone else there to offer advice, someone we can trust to be mature and to have our children's best interests at heart.

Those of us who don't have extended family nearby or who unfortunately don't get along with our own families can still build a network of friends who can help care for and watch over our children. In one of my parenting seminars, a woman told the group about such an experience. "After my mother died, one of her friends began to visit my family," she said. "We had just had a baby, and my mom's friend, who didn't have grandchildren, fell in love with our daughter. Through her presence, I felt a strong connection to my mother and was grateful for her visits. This was a mutual 'adoption' that has continued throughout my daughter's childhood."

Close connections with family and friends outside the

nuclear family open up our children's world. An extended network of loving adults can help create a richer world for our children—one that inspires their curiosity, suggests exciting possibilities beyond the realm of the everyday, and provides them with the advantage of knowing that adults other than their parents believe in them. Since every individual has unique talents and perspectives to offer, the more caring adults who are actively involved in our children's lives, the better off they will be.

Celebrating the Family

Family celebrations are really important for kids. As the clan gathers, and the children play together, the grown-ups exclaim over how they've grown, how smart they are, how beautiful, how strong. The kids, of course, are embarrassed by all the fuss, but the message that they are loved, treasured, and admired sinks in, even as they run off to play again.

As they grow older, taking part in these gatherings will help them develop a deep-rooted sense of belonging that will serve them well as they move out from home and family to explore the world. Family gatherings are a time for ritual, when our cultural and ethnic traditions are celebrated, and when we tell stories about the past. Children love to hear about our childhood escapades. Through these stories, they learn important new things about us, and they get a valuable peek into that long-ago time when we were children. The stories can also help them develop a sense of the changes that come with time, and give meaning to the abstract notion that just as their parents once were children, one day they will be parents.

Family celebrations can also give our children a chance to see us as people, not just parents, by revealing us in a new and different light. They are surprised, even thrilled, when we do something unexpected: take off our shoes and dance to oldies music, never bothering them about their bedtime, for example. Life becomes a party!

After one family gathering, Billy asks his father on the way home, "Did you know you're Mikey's favorite uncle?"

Dad smiles, "Yeah, I guess I knew that," he says.

"Boy, was I surprised!" Billy says. Seeing how important his dad is in the eyes of his favorite cousin gives Billy a new respect for his father, too.

Family gatherings at holidays also give children a way of understanding the passage of time and the fact that they are growing up. Often, pictures are taken at these events, and especially if they are annual gatherings, our children can look at the pictures and see how much they've grown since the last time. Sometimes it's fun to take pictures of the new generation, using the composition of favorite old family photographs as a model. Both children and adults enjoy setting up the poses, and comparing the pictures when they are developed.

Family celebrations can also be a time when we perform family rituals that may be passed down from generation to generation. At my family gatherings, for example, we light candles for those who are unable to be present. We hold hands around the table and have a moment of quiet blessing, when we think warm thoughts about our absent loved ones, before proceeding with the meal.

Celebrating the Everyday

We don't always need to wait for a holiday to enjoy a festive atmosphere. Sometimes invoking the holiday spirit can turn a dreary day into a memorable occasion.

It's nearing the end of Christmas vacation, and Mom is trying to think of what to do with her four kids and their visiting cousin who have tired of their new toys, are getting on each other's nerves, and are sick of the frigid weather. "I have an idea," she says one night. "Let's have a beach party!" The kids, who range in age from four to eleven, look at her as though she is crazy.

"Are you kidding?" the oldest asks.

"No, I'm not. Let's start planning it," Mom answers, and starts making a list of menu ideas and things to bring.

"But it's freezing outside," one child protests.

"We'll have our beach party indoors," Mom replies. "We'll tan by the light of the lamp."

The kids get into the spirit of the idea and start discussing what to wear, which toys to bring, which CDs to listen to, and of course, what to eat—and Mom promises to get hot dogs and the fixings for s'mores.

The next day is very cold, but Mom turns up the thermostat and Dad lights a fire in the fireplace of the family room. Everybody helps push the furniture back to make room for the beach blankets and the cooler. Dad opens up the beach umbrella, blows up a beach ball, puts a Beach Boys CD on the stereo and the scene is set. The kids put on their bathing suits and sunglasses, and slather on sweet-smelling tanning lotion, giggling all the while. They have a great time roasting and toasting their food, using coat hangers as skewers. They laugh, play, and dance together. When the "beach party" is over and they are "home" again, the kids talk about how much they enjoyed their trip out of the everyday routine. The eleven-year-old says, "That was awesome," and the youngest asks eagerly, "Can we do it again tomorrow?"

It's important for our children to know that they can have fun with their families. We don't want them to feel they always have to look for good times elsewhere. When our young children learn that laughter, fun, warmth, and closeness are all part of family life, they will enjoy spending time with us. This will reverberate into the future, near and far. When our kids begin testing their independence as teenagers, they will be more likely to come to us for advice and conversation. And when they start a family of their own, they will know how to create new family traditions.

Linking the Past With the Future

The general tone of our everyday lives together will affect our children's memories of family life. These experiences and relationships will go with them into their relationships, their marriages, their own families, and their futures as a whole.

As I've said so many times, it is what we do with our children that counts, much more than what we say or even what we believe. Our values are transmitted across the generations through our behavior. Our children witness and absorb the way we live together day to day, and what they learn serves as a model for them all their lives, affecting not only them, but their children. We can think of our loving actions as a kind of chain of love that stretches both forward and back across the generations.

Giving our children a world filled with encouragement, tolerance, and praise; a world in which they receive our acceptance, approval, and recognition; a world where they can share honestly and expect fairness, kindness, and consideration in return, can make a real difference in their lives and in the quality of life for everyone around them.

Let's expect the best of our children—and in fact, of all children: the kids down the street, the kids across town, kids far away. Let's do all we can to make it easy for them to do their best. After all, it's our neighborhood, our town, our country, our planet. Let's do what we can to ensure that our children will be part of a future that gradually eliminates fear, hunger, prejudice, and intolerance—a future that includes the acceptance of every person on our planet into the family of mankind.

Let's pave the way for our children to see the world in the best light, so that they'll find it—and can help make it—a nice place to live.